# SECRET
# SONOMA

## A Guide to the Weird, Wonderful, and Obscure

Karen Misuraca

Reedy Press
PO Box 5131
St. Louis, MO 63139
www.reedypress.com

Library of Congress Control Number: 2021935142
ISBN: 9781681063386

Design by Jill Halpin

Unless otherwise indicated, all photos are courtesy of the author or in the public domain.

Printed in the United States of America
21 22 23 24 25   5 4 3 2 1

To my tireless cheerleader, Michael, and to my daughters, grandkids, and great grandboy, all of whom are avid explorers of the weird and wonderful curiosities of Sonoma County.

# CONTENTS

# INTRODUCTION

As a lifelong resident of Sonoma County, I know the hidden gardens, the little-known museums, the historic sites, and the glories of the rugged coastline and the wine valleys. Nonetheless, while researching this book for you, I discovered some delightful oddities that I didn't know existed.

More than just a pretty place with great wine and redwood trees, this green and golden region of Northern California runs the gamut from rustic roadhouses to Victorian mansions, NASCAR to slot cars, from a *Star Wars* museum to a bicycle built for 12, an African safari, and a beer-lovers cult.

We're loaded with history here too. We've got the last-built California mission, vintage fighter jets, a Mexican general (the influencer of his time), and traces of our indigenous forefathers. We go ziplining, grape stomping, hiking with cows, and glamping at the river (when we're not wading around in tide pools).

Whether you're a visitor or you've lived here all your life as I have, as you page through the guide, you're bound to be surprised at the wonders you come across if you just knew where to look— and now you do!

As Dr. Seuss said, "We are all a little weird, and life's a little weird."

# ACKNOWLEDGMENTS

Many, many thanks to the people, organizations, and businesses that helped and encouraged me during these months of research and discovery, through which all of us carried on steadfastly amid a year of setbacks and sadness. I feel like I'm back, and Sonoma County is definitely back, better than ever.

I could not have produced *Secret Sonoma* without my daughter, Jessica, my main reader and editor, and my husband, Michael— always my #1 cheerleader and guardian. Another Reedy Press author, Yvonne Horn, so generously shared her experience at our frequent pep talks, and colleagues from the Bay Area Travel Writers stepped up, as usual, with good advice and inspiration.

Even though I love and know it so well, I never imagined that Sonoma County would reveal such a rich well of history and more glorious countryside and coastline than I knew existed. Above all, I met so many welcoming, quirky, funny, and fun inhabitants, of both the two-footed and four-footed variety.

Now I know why when I say I'm from Sonoma, people always say, "Oh, aren't you lucky!"

# WIND BENEATH YOUR WINGS

## Where can we relive the golden age of flight?

Founded in 1946 when it was known as Aeroschelleville, Sonoma Valley Airport is a living history museum of classic and antique aircraft. Just imagine yourself as the Red Baron in the 450-horsepower, bright red, open-cockpit 1942 Stearman. This one and the other two Stearman biplanes here have been modified to accommodate two passengers and the pilot.

Armed with a mouthful of sharp teeth on its fuselage, the fighter and ground-attack P-40 Warhawk was the model that the Flying Tigers, our pilots, and our allies flew in World War II, while the royal blue, Navy version of the AT-6 Texan is what our fighter pilots trained in during World War II. You can catch a ride in these perfectly restored, historic planes either by booking ahead or by dropping in on weekends. If you want to stay on the ground, just come by and take selfies with these photogenic beauties.

Rides are thrilling in the open-air planes, from a quick, exhilarating 20-minute thriller to a longer flyover of wine country. Other choices are the "West to the Pacific" tour, and the unforgettable "Spires of

## HOME OF THE TAIL DRAGGERS

**WHAT:** Rare vintage aircraft on display and for open-cockpit rides

**WHERE:** 23982 Arnold Dr./Hwy. 121, Sonoma

**COST:** Free to see. For flights, $174 to $799 depending on the plane and the tour; for $50 extra, get aerobatics such as the loop, barrel roll, and hammerhead.

**PRO TIP:** When NASCAR, NHRA, and other big race days are scheduled at Sonoma Raceway nearby, there may be gridlock traffic on Hwy. 121; check for dates at sonomaraceway.com.

*The open-cockpit biplane PT-17 Stearman was used for military training in the 1930s and 1940s. After World War II, surplus Stearmans were sold for use as crop dusters and for aerobatics and wing-walking in air shows. Left and inset photos courtesy of Sonoma Valley Airport*

The City" flight toward San Francisco Bay and the Golden Gate Bridge that takes you over Sausalito, Mt. Tamalpais, and Point Reyes National Seashore. If you've got a hankering to see your words in the wild blue yonder, you can arrange for the skywriting of what you've always wanted to say!

It's free to see the vintage aircraft at the small airport. In addition, Display Days are held the second weekend of each month, when all the gleaming biplanes are on parade.

# CALL OF THE WILD

## Where is the ghost of Jack London?

In the early 20th century, the world-renowned author of adventure novels, Jack London, retreated to the hills of Sonoma Valley to become a rancher and to build a gargantuan stone mansion, "Wolf House," in a redwood and pine forest. In 1913, after two years of construction, the 15,000-square-foot, castle-like edifice was finally complete, with 26 rooms, a reflection pool, a huge library, nine fireplaces, and a wine cellar. And then one night, the mansion was destroyed in a heartbreaking inferno, said to have started in a pile of oily rags.

Only the thick stone walls remained, as they do today, in Jack London State Historic Park. From a high boardwalk, you can look down into the tragic ruin above massive archways, the empty pool, and the yawning fireplaces, and imagine how Jack's dream house would have echoed to house parties, and how he would have click-clacked away on his 1902 Bar Lock #10 typewriter.

Despairing and unable financially to rebuild, London spent the last three years of his life writing—and, they say, drinking—in a small, circa-1860s cottage, which is now a museum filled with memorabilia and vintage photos. Jack's wife, Charmian, wrote, "The razing of his house killed something in Jack, and he never ceased to feel the tragic inner sense of loss."

A much larger museum in the park is in the "House of Happy Walls," built by Charmian after Jack's death in 1916. As well as showcasing his novel writing and journalistic career, fascinating

Set in the wilderness of Alaska, London's best-known novels are *The Sea Wolf*, *Call of the Wild*, and *White Fang*.

## JACK LONDON STATE HISTORIC PARK

**WHAT:** Wolf House at Jack London State Historic Park

**WHERE:** 2400 London Ranch Rd., Glen Ellen

**COST:** $10 per vehicle

**PRO TIP:** In the summertime, in open-air winery ruins in the park, Transcendence Theatre's *Broadway Under the Stars* is performed by real Broadway singers and dancers.

Top left: *Surrounded by thousands of acres of Jack London State Historic Park the "House of Happy Walls" is an interactive museum of London's yachting adventures in the South Pacific and his novel writing and journalistic career.*

Bottom left and right: *Just as Jack London's monumental "Wolf House" mansion was completed in 1913, it burned to the ground. The poignant and spectacular ruins are just one of the historic landmarks in Jack London State Park. All photos courtesy of Jack London State Park*

displays depict their voyage to the South Pacific on their yacht, the *Snark*. The historic sites are surrounded by thousands of acres of Jack London State Historic Park, where you can hike, ride horses, and picnic.

# LANDFILL TO LANDMARK

## What's a cow doing in that red pickup truck?

Why are those tin cans riding in a fire truck, and is that a sharkmobile? Is that Babe Ruth I see? Get out your camera and go for a stroll down Florence Avenue, the coolest street in Sebastopol—and maybe the coolest street in the county. In front yards and on porches are dozens of funky, vividly colorful, whimsical "junk art" creations made by local sculptor Patrick Amiot out of old headlights, bicycles, tires, oil cans, car parts, and anything else that can be dug out of a dumpster. Among his more than 100 street sculptures in town are a dog with a mailbox nose, a surfer girl with speedometer eyes, and a milkman with a trash can torso.

Amiot creates miracles by recycling metal, ceramic, wood, and myriad cast-off materials into quirky, fun works of art.

A constantly changing parade of quirky characters enlivens the front yard of the Amiot's 1909 bungalow at 382 Florence. If you're lucky, you'll be there on an open studio day when Patrick

**JUNK ART**

**WHAT:** Spectacular junk art creations around Sebastopol and beyond

**WHERE:** Florence Ave. and environs, Sebastopol

**COST:** Free

**PRO TIP:** Stop by the Community Market to see one of Amiot's Black Lives Matter junk artworks.

One of Amiot's most spectacular installations, the 50-feet-wide "Pride of Canada" carousel in Markham, Canada, is a whirling collection of 44 whimsical, outrageous, rideable creatures.

*Inhabiting the streets of Sebastopol and beyond, whimsical, vividly colorful "junk art" characters are created by the artist Patrick Amiot from recycled vehicles, bike parts, tin cans, wooden boxes, dumpster finds, and castoffs. Photos courtesy of Patrick Amiot*

and his wife, Brigitte, welcome visitors, hand out tour maps, and sell the sculptures. Brigitte actually does most of the painting of the fabulous creations.

Around Sebastopol and other towns in the county, when you see a wonderful, photogenic concoction, it may well be an Amiot creation; many are electrified, making for zany nighttime outings.

# A GHOSTLY FOREST

## Is that you, Charles Darwin?

Along the footpath to the Buena Vista Winery, shadowy, life-sized figures appear among the oak trees on the hillside—Osiris, Egyptian god of wine; Dionysus, Greek god of wine; a trio of our founding fathers (Washington, Jefferson, and Franklin); and a bevy of wine-industry titans, early explorers, and other luminaries from the past century or so. Some of these two-dimensional, faded apparitions have raised their arms and seem about to walk down the hill, while others stand as classic statuary in their togas. Charles Darwin and Thomas Edison hold forth here on "History Hill" beneath the branches, along with Padre Jose Altimira, exhausted, no doubt, after planting the first vineyard in what is now the California Wine Country. Lifting a glass is the "Father of the California Viticulture," Count Agoston Haraszthy, founder of Buena Vista Winery in 1857.

## HISTORY HILL AT BUENA VISTA WINERY

**WHAT:** Ghostly presences on History Hill

**WHERE:** Buena Vista Winery, 18000 Old Winery Rd., Sonoma

**COST:** Free to see; fees for wine tasting and tours

**PRO TIP:** At the winery, you may encounter a gregarious and convincing impersonator of the Count in full costume, presenting a living history experience in the museum and at special events.

Nearby, Bartholomew Estate was the site of the first privately owned vineyard in the valley, planted in 1832. Linger here for wine tasting, picnicking, and trail hiking.

Top left: *Ghosts of harvests past, the Franciscan Father Jose Altimira planted the first vineyards in today's wine country and built Mission San Francisco Solano, while in the Mexican occupation of the 1830s, General Mariano Vallejo laid out the town of Sonoma.*

Top right: *Holding forth on History Hill as the "Plant Wizard" of horticultural fame, Luther Burbank developed hundreds of varieties of fruits, flowers, and grains in the 1880s.*

Bottom right: *At the entrance to Buena Vista Winery, Washington, Jefferson, and Franklin find themselves amid the oaks in the faded mists of time.*

Across the path from History Hill, take a wander through The Maze, a hedge-lined labyrinth dotted with signposts describing Haraszthy's life and innovative viticulture. Beyond the ghosts and the maze is a historic landmark, Buena Vista Winery, which is a compound of impressive stone buildings, a museum, ornate wine tasting venues done up in antiques and fine art, and picnic sites. It's free to come in and explore the two-story Press House, where peacocks named "I Am Pinot Noir" and "I Am Pinot Mernier" are gracefully draped amid the historic artifacts.

# STARSTRUCK AT SUGARLOAF

## Where can I see the stars?

Far from city lights at the top of Sugarloaf Ridge State Park in Sonoma Valley sits a 40-inch reflector telescope, the largest in the western United States devoted entirely to public viewing and education. A rare and valuable local asset, the all-volunteer-operated Robert Ferguson Observatory also has two other powerful telescopes available to visitors: a robotic, 20-inch research-grade charge-coupled device (CCD) telescope and an 8-inch refractor telescope. Each year's lively calendar offers classes and live presentations in the teaching lab; wildly popular, docent-led star parties; and more astronomy events. You can learn all about pulsars, star life cycles, constellations, globular clusters, black holes, and all the mysteries of galaxies, nebulae, the Milky Way, and beyond.

Night sky viewing is so clear up here that star gazers, scientists, and astronomy enthusiasts gather on many crystalline nights, when you can see a carpet of millions of stars even without a telescope. For laser-guided constellation tours without telescopes, sign up for "Night Sky Trails" star parties and the "Bring Your Own Binoculars and Chair" evenings; be aware that the park's nearby campground does fill up on those magical nights.

---

Walk from the sun to Pluto on the 4.5-mile PlanetWalk, a scale model of the solar system to "see" each of the plants. Every step you take crosses a million miles of empty space.

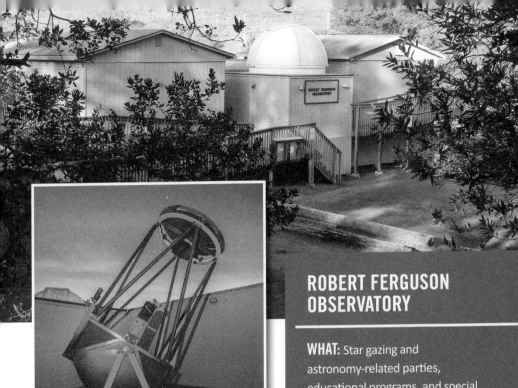

*Weighing a third of a ton, the 40-inch reflecting telescope at the Robert Ferguson Observatory is the largest in the western US devoted to public viewing. Frequent star parties and astronomy events are topped off annually by Dark Sky Week in April. Photos courtesy of Robert Ferguson Observatory*

## ROBERT FERGUSON OBSERVATORY

**WHAT:** Star gazing and astronomy-related parties, educational programs, and special events at one of the largest observatories in the West

**WHERE:** Sugarloaf Ridge State Park in Sonoma Valley, 5 minutes from Hwy. 12, 2605 Adobe Canyon Rd., Kenwood

**COST:** Star parties are $3; free for those under 18. Other events are affordably priced. An $8 parking fee is charged in the State Park.

**PRO TIP:** Book a private star-viewing party with two gregarious astronomers from Wine County Star Party— perhaps a romantic date night, a gala wine-and-food evening, a special birthday, or just to assemble your new telescope and learn how to use it.

Exciting events are scheduled during Dark Sky Week in April. Daytime solar observations are free, when two solar telescopes are available for safe observation of that fiery globe. Who knew you could look directly at the sun?

# REMEMBERING THE *SNARK*

## What are those fine little boats doing in the creek?

In the village of Glen Ellen just down the hill from Jack London State Historic Park, Sonoma Creek burbles merrily along beneath a canopy of oak trees. Some of the more eccentric of local Jack London aficionados pay homage to the adventure novelist with an annual Jack to Jack Yacht Race in the creek, when the waters are high and fast-moving in April.

Just for the race, every year, model boats are hand-crafted out of wood from redwood trees recovered from the catastrophic fires near here in 2017. These charming little yachts are 18-inch-long replicas of London's oceangoing vessel, the *Snark*, on which he set sail from Oakland in 1907 on a voyage to the South Pacific.

History lovers, merrymakers, and fundraisers for local nonprofit organizations, members of the Jack London Yacht Club base the race at the circa-1905 Jack London Lodge Saloon, from where they launch their flotilla of sailboats on a .7-mile course down the creek, from the lodge to Jack London Village.

Cameras are placed along the banks of the creek and GPS is installed in each boat, allowing spectators to watch the race live at the lodge or at home. Volunteer firefighters release

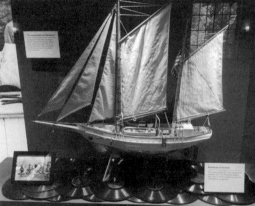

Top left: *The iconic author of such adventure novels as* Call of the Wild, White Fang, *and* The Sea Wolf, *Jack London is celebrated annually at the Jack to Jack Yacht Race in Glen Ellen. Photo courtesy of the Jack London Yacht Club*

Top right: *The Jack to Jack race headquarters is in the circa-1850s Jack London Lodge and Saloon, where diners and yachties gather on the creek side deck. Photo courtesy of Sonoma County Tourism*

Bottom right: *In the Jack London State Historic Park museum, a model of the* Snark, *the ketch that London sailed to the South Pacific in 1907.*

and catch the boats, helping to resolve finish-line squabbles, as several competitive races ensue. The winners are draped in leis, in remembrance of London's arrival in Hawaii on the *Snark*. Live entertainment rocks the beer garden on the creekside deck at the lodge, where food and wine are abundant for competitors and spectators.

All year long, locals belly up to the antique bar at the Saloon at Jack London Lodge, watching sports on TV, playing pool, and enjoying local wines and a menu of hearty grub on the creekside deck.

# BELLY UP TO THE BAR

## Who fought the Battle of Washoe House?

On a stagecoach route connecting Sonoma County towns in the 1860s, the Washoe House saloon and dance hall was patronized by gold rush miners, gamblers, wagon drivers, and women of colorful repute. This roadhouse and several others in the county are still welcoming merrymakers . . . these days, of rather higher moral character.

In 1865, enraged by Lincoln's assassination, the "Emmett Rifles" local militiamen rode and marched from Petaluma toward Santa Rosa to take their revenge against the *Santa Rosa Democrat* newspaper, known to favor the South.

Thirsty and dusty, the marauders stopped along the way for libations at Washoe House, where they settled in at

### WASHOE HOUSE

**WHAT:** A raucous history and brews on tap at an old stagecoach stop

**WHERE:** 2840 Roblar Rd., Petaluma

**COST:** Free to see

**PRO TIP:** Enjoy live country music on weekends and karaoke some Wednesday nights.

One of the oldest roadhouses in the West, opened in 1854, Stormy's is the only remaining business in what was the gold rush–era village of Bloomfield. Dairy ranchers, winemakers, and locals in the know come here for prime rib, fried chicken, clam chowder, and brews by the fireplace in the bar.

*Today's Washoe House and other roadhouses and stagecoach stops from the 1800s still welcome thirsty travelers for beer on tap and rollicking good times at the bar; these days, gourmet grub and live music are on the menu, too. Photo courtesy of Sonoma County Tourism*

the long bar, which seemed like a better idea than marauding. Known since then as the "Battle of Washoe House" that never happened, the caper added to the gaudy history of the place that is today recalled on the ceiling, which is covered with old photos, thousands of dollar bills, and memorabilia from decades gone by. Scenes in the 1999 Clint Eastwood movie, *True Crime*, were filmed here.

A popular watering hole and eatery today as ever, Washoe House rides the outer reaches of Roblar Road in red clapboard glory above rolling hills dotted with dairy cows. Pickup trucks share the parking lot with Harleys and snazzy sports cars.

# THE NICHOLAS EFFECT

## How did a seven-year-old save so many lives?

Drifting out over the surrounding meadows and hillsides in the soft sea air, 140 bells chime on the Children's Bell Tower near Bodega Bay. Dedicated to all children, the 18-foot-tall, three-tiered monument is a memorial to Nicholas Green, a seven-year-old who was shot and killed by robbers while on a family vacation in Italy in 1994.

When the Green family donated his organs and corneas to seven Italians who were awaiting transplants, the Italians responded in a wave of love and appreciation that resulted in a dramatic increase in organ donations and donor pledges in that country and beyond, a phenomenon called l'*Effetto Nicholas* (the Nicholas Effect). For the monument—a series of pyramids from which hang the bells—families, schools, churches, and other organizations sent beautiful school bells, church bells, ships' bells, mining bells, and cowbells. In the center is a 30-inch-high bell from the Marinelli foundry in Italy, which made bells for the papacy for centuries. John Paul II blessed the bell, upon which is engraved Nicholas's

### CHILDREN'S BELL TOWER

**WHAT:** A moving memorial to a young boy whose loss transformed the organ donation campaign in Italy

**WHERE:** 2255 CA-1, Bodega Bay

**COST:** Free

**PRO TIP:** April is National Donate Life Month, a campaign to encourage people to register to donate organs, eyes, and tissue.

From the Bell Tower, the Coastal Prairie Trail is a 1.1-mile walking trail to Salmon Creek beach, with meadow and sea views.

*Bells echo softly in sea breezes off the Pacific, on a moving memorial to a young boy who died tragically, only to leave a legacy of hope for seven people who live and thrive due to his family's generosity. Photos courtesy of The Nicholas Green Foundation*

name and the names of the seven organ recipients. Nicholas's hometown of Bodega Bay arranged the building of the tower, and the Italian Air Force transported the Italian bells to California.

A copse of cypress trees shelters the setting, which looks onto rolling hills, sand dunes, and ocean views. When the sea winds blow, which they often do, the bell chimes create a miraculous symphony of joyful music.

One of the recipients of Nicholas's organs was 19-year-old Maria Pia, who today is now married, with two children, one of whom she named Nicholas.

# HANGING OUT WITH *PEANUTS*

## Where are you, Charlie Brown?

Santa Rosa is the hometown of the *Peanuts* comic strip characters and of Charles Schulz, their beloved creator. You can't fail to notice that Snoopy, Charlie Brown, Lucy, Linus, Woodstock, and even Schroeder are seen all around the town and the county. They're everywhere—at the airport, at the golf courses, on street corners and in parks, at hospitals, and beyond—more than 100 larger-than-life-sized bronze, ceramic, and fiberglass statues of the *Peanuts* kids.

Their creator, the late cartoonist Charles Schulz (aka "Sparky") lived and worked here for decades. He was a beloved resident and generous contributor to the community, from building an ice arena to funding the Charles M. Schulz Museum.

Four characters are helping out at the Charles M. Schultz Sonoma County Airport: Lucy offers her 5 cents, Charlie Brown gives directions to check-in, Snoopy stands tall in his pilot's helmet, and Woodstock is perched on his nest. Lucy's "Airport Help" desk is ready to serve as well. Several of the gang are at Kaiser Medical Center, including Woodstock reading *The Life of a Bird*, and at other hospitals and local businesses, shopping centers, hotels, and more.

At the Railroad Square former railroad depot, Charlie Brown and Snoopy stand in elegant bronze splendor, over the

---

The largest group of *Peanuts* kids is at the Flamingo Resort, where Charlie Brown and Snoopy wear Giants baseball uniforms autographed by players, and Snoopy holds court in an Egyptian-style headdress.

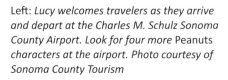

Left: *Lucy welcomes travelers as they arrive and depart at the Charles M. Schulz Sonoma County Airport. Look for four more* Peanuts *characters at the airport. Photo courtesy of Sonoma County Tourism*

Right: *Charlie Brown greets travelers with a smile at the Charles M. Schulz Sonoma County Airport. Photo courtesy of Charles Schulz Museum*

Inset: *Charlie Brown in his Rastafarian days, now hanging out at the Montgomery Village Shopping Center.*

## PEANUTS CHARACTERS

**WHAT:** The characters from the *Peanuts* comic strip

**WHERE:** Many locations throughout Santa Rosa and the county

**COST:** Free

**PRO TIP:** At the Warm Puppy Café in the Redwood Empire Ice Arena (Snoopy's Home Ice), enjoy hot dogs and ice cream while watching the action on the ice. As Charlie Brown said, "Happiness is a warm puppy."

plaque that reads: "In celebration of the life and works of Charles M. Schulz from the people of Santa Rosa and his fans across the world." Here also at the California Welcome Center, Lucy is decked out in her official outfit for welcoming tourists.

# MARINE SCIENCE ON VIEW

## Where can we take our budding marine biologist?

Get your family hooked on the wonders of the sea with a visit to the Bodega Marine Laboratory at Bodega Bay, operated by the University of California, Davis, since the 1960s. Half a mile of county coastline and marine environment is protected and studied here by students, who welcome visitors and conduct fascinating tours of research projects.

Sea life along the coast is on view in a 24-foot-long display containing local fish and a kelp forest. The harbor aquarium showcases the sea life of Bodega Harbor, while another aquarium is the home of giant anemones and other organisms that you might encounter in tide pools along this coastline. In addition, a 5,000-gallon outdoor tide pool is alive with sea creatures.

---

### BODEGA BAY MARINE LABORATORY

**WHAT:** Immerse yourself in the exciting world of marine science right at the water's edge.

**WHERE:** 2099 Westshore Rd., Bodega Bay

**COST:** Free

**PRO TIP:** Ask about the Ocean Observing Node!

---

If you see scuba divers on the shore, they are scientists learning to dive safely while conducting ocean research around the world.

Top: *Students of marine biology explain tide pool specimens in the several aquariums at the Marine Lab in Bodega Bay.*

Inset: *Pacific Coast sea creatures are studied and exhibited at the UC Davis marine science center in Bodega Bay.*
*Photos courtesy of the Bodega Marine Laboratory*

The students will explain the many experiments they're working on, as well as how climate change and acidification of the oceans are affecting marine life. They are also studying oysters, kelp, and salt marsh restoration; aqua farming; invasive species such as sea urchins; and more oceanographic science.

You may be lucky enough to get a glimpse of one or more of their high-tech floating research vessels from which they collect deep-water corals and sediment cores full of mysterious fossils.

# FLYING IN THE TREETOPS

## Okay, whose idea was it to go ziplining?

At 250 feet above the ground, fearless adventurers get a bird's-eye view of an ancient California coast redwood forest (not too scary, as 10-year-olds are often seen flying between the trees). The Sonoma Canopy Tours expedition involves soaring over a mile on multiple ziplines connected by platforms; climbing a steep, spiral staircase; and balancing on eight suspended "sky bridges," ending in a three-story rappel back down to mother earth. On a guided, 2.5-hour tour, in a harness attached to a pulley on a heavy steel cable, you'll soar through and above the trees and deep ravines at speeds of between 25 and 40 miles an hour! Don't worry, though, you can practice on a small course before braving the ziplines.

Throughout the exhilarating experience of getting up close to some of the tallest and oldest living trees on earth, naturalist guides impart details of the complex and endangered coast redwood ecosystem and

## SONOMA CANOPY TOURS

**WHAT:** Thrilling zipline tours high up in a coast redwood forest

**WHERE:** 6250 Bohemian Hwy., Occidental

**COST:** $99 to $139 per person

**PRO TIP:** Stargazing after dark from the skyscraper-high platforms and ziplines is dreamlike on the Night Flight Tour.

About 82% of the remaining, endangered ancient coast redwood forests are protected in parks and reserves.

Top: *Amid the ziplines and the sky bridges, glamping is camping with style in a yurt in the Treehouse Grove.*

Inset: *Thrilling ziplining adventures at 25 miles an hour in a coast redwood forest. Photos courtesy of Sonoma Canopy Tours*

the endangered and threatened wildlife, especially birdlife, that depend on this habitat.

This is a busy place every day of the year, even in the rainy season when mists and raindrops float through the redwoods, creating a magical atmosphere. Rain or shine, you can stay overnight in the Treehouse Grove in a sturdy, round yurt-style cabin in the tree canopy. Sleeping four, it's nicely furnished with en suite facilities, and dinner and breakfast are included.

# HISTORIC HEART OF SONOMA

## Where is the last California mission?

Founded in 1824, the crown jewel of Sonoma State Historic Park, and the last and northernmost of the 21 mission churches in Alta California, Mission San Francisco Solano de Sonoma was constructed by Coast Miwok and other indigenous people, as well as a contingent of Mexican soldiers. You'll know you're there when you see a massive prickly pear cactus at the entry door.

No longer a Catholic church, the mission today is a simpler version, architecturally, of the original. Inside are religious and history-related works of art, paintings of most of the California missions, re-created rooms, costumes of the early days, and a sweet chapel that sees the occasional wedding. The tall bell tower is long gone, although there is a large bell dating from the early 1800s, which was stolen mid-century and then recovered in 1910.

Among annual events at the mission are candlelit musicals in the chapel at Christmastime, costumed reenactments of the 1846 Bear Flag Revolt, and the weddings of the daughters of the Mexican General Vallejo to the sons of Count Agoston Haraszthy, "Father of California Viticulture."

Across from the mission, the lovely, rather decrepit adobe building is one of the oldest in the state. Within the two-foot-thick walls of the Blue Wing Inn was a saloon and gambling hall frequented by gold rush–era miners and billeted US army soldiers.

## SONOMA STATE HISTORIC PARK

**WHAT:** Mission San Francisco Solano de Sonoma

**WHERE:** Corner of East Spain and First Street East, Sonoma

**COST:** $3 for adults, $2 for ages 6–16, free for children under 5. Tickets are good on the same day for the multisite Sonoma State Historic Park in Sonoma and the Petaluma Adobe.

**PRO TIP:** The gift shop offers items related to California history and lots of toys and educational things for kids.

Top: *A monument to 18th- and 19th-century California history, Mission San Francisco Solano de Sonoma is the northernmost of the 21 California missions built during the Spanish and Mexican eras. Photo courtesy of Visit California*

Inset: *Ringing throughout downtown Sonoma on special occasions, the iron bell at the Sonoma mission dates from the early 1800s; stolen in mid-century, it was recovered in 1910.*

A monument outside the church honors more than 900 native people—from Coast Miwok, Pomo, Suisunes, Wappo, and Patwin tribes—who died while living and working at the mission between 1824 and 1839, primarily due to European diseases such as measles and smallpox.

# MOVIE MAVENS' WINERY

## Swimmin' and sippin' and goin' to the movies

One of the many "only in Sonoma County" attractions is the Francis Ford Coppola Winery, entirely unique not only here, but on the planet. The gem of the museum-like collection of movie memorabilia on display is the ruby-red 1948 Tucker automobile from Coppola's late 1980s film, *Tucker: The Man and His Dream*. *Apocalypse Now* gets its own exhibit as does *Dracula*. Look for the Godfather's desk, a plethora of Oscars, and war ships from daughter Sofia Coppola's film, *Marie Antoinette*.

Found at no other winery are two swimming pools, a festive line-up of poolside cabanas and lounge chairs (open to the public by reservation), game tables, bocce courts, and a wine and snacks pavilion. Inspired by the bandshell in *The Godfather: Part II*, with the original mural from the film, the outdoor stage hosts live entertainment such as "Dancing Under the Stars" and "Swimming Under the Stars," when guests float, nosh, sip, and kick up their heels beneath the summer moon (adults only).

Surrounded by two floors of luxury gift items are wine-tasting salons where oenophiles ask for the "Apocalypse Now" red blend; daughter Sofia's own sparkling wine;

## FRANCIS FORD COPPOLA WINERY

**WHAT:** A movie museum, outdoor fun, and fine wines at a movie mogul's fantasy winery

**WHERE:** 300 Via Archimedes, Geyserville

**COST:** Free to see; wine tasting $30 and up

**PRO TIP:** Coppola was the first to popularize fine wine in a can, with the Sofia Blanc de Blancs in 2004, which is perfect for wine country picnics.

*Unique among wineries for its resort-like estate, Francis Ford Coppola Winery is all about movie memorabilia, a swimming pool open to the public, and fine wines. Photo courtesy of Sonoma County Tourism*

the Archimedes Cabernet; an homage to Coppola's Uncle Archimedes; Director's Cut Cabernet, and dozens more varietals. Food and wine pairing ensues at the restaurant, Rustic, where patrons tuck into meats grilled on the authentic Argentine *parrilla*, while enjoying glorious views of the Alexander Valley.

Nearby, visit the Victorian village of Geyserville, where fancy 19th-century mansions take pride of place alongside eateries and wine-tasting salons.

# NO NUKES ON THIS COAST

## What's that hole in the Head?

The Bodega Head, that is. In the 1960s, this rugged, legendary coastline came close to having a massive nuclear power facility perched smack on the headlands above Bodega Bay, about two miles from the San Andreas Fault (think earthquake). Years of antinuke uproar and community activism caused the Kennedy administration to take notice, and a negative review by the Atomic Energy Commission forced the power company to cancel its plan. Reflective of the protests that led to the demise of the plan, 1,500 helium balloons were released, each with the words "This balloon could represent a radioactive molecule of strontium 90 or iodine 131." The antinuke sentiment also birthed the antinuclear movement that ultimately protected the entire California coast. Before the plant was canceled, a giant pit was dug near the tip of Bodega Head; today, it's a pond called Hole in the Head.

While enjoying the stunning views of the seacoast from the breezy walking paths high above Bodega Bay, you can see the hole, now a resting spot for migratory birds. You'll likely also see seals and sea lions, some of 150 species of birds, and sea otters floating in the kelp beds. Binoculars are handy to see the raptors, egrets, herons, and the endangered Western snowy plover up close.

Bodega Head is on the Pacific tectonic plate, while the town of Bodega sits on the North American plate; between them is the often-shifting, 800-mile-long San Andreas Fault.

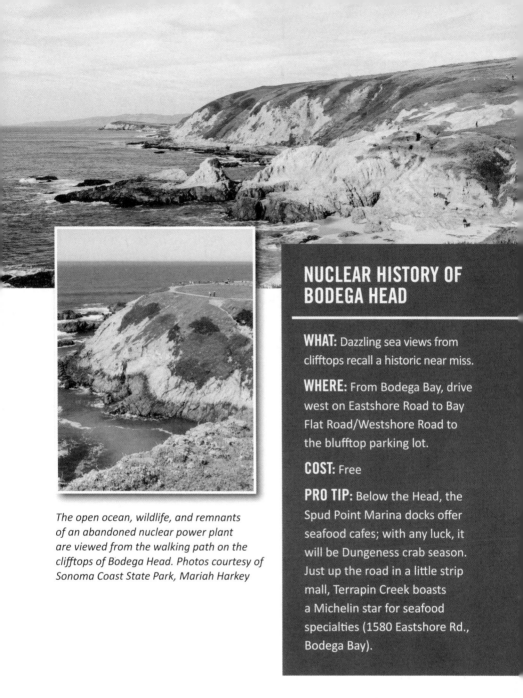

## NUCLEAR HISTORY OF BODEGA HEAD

**WHAT:** Dazzling sea views from clifftops recall a historic near miss.

**WHERE:** From Bodega Bay, drive west on Eastshore Road to Bay Flat Road/Westshore Road to the blufftop parking lot.

**COST:** Free

**PRO TIP:** Below the Head, the Spud Point Marina docks offer seafood cafes; with any luck, it will be Dungeness crab season. Just up the road in a little strip mall, Terrapin Creek boasts a Michelin star for seafood specialties (1580 Eastshore Rd., Bodega Bay).

*The open ocean, wildlife, and remnants of an abandoned nuclear power plant are viewed from the walking path on the clifftops of Bodega Head. Photos courtesy of Sonoma Coast State Park, Mariah Harkey*

A 1.7-mile East Trail loops south above the open ocean, while the West Trail loop runs west for 1.2 miles above Horseshoe Cove with a 265-foot-high perch from which to spot migrating gray whales swimming near the shoreline from December to April on their way south to Mexico.

# SAVING ENDANGERED FLORA

## What is a horticultural ark?

Just as Noah gathered the world's animals onto his ark to save them from the flood, thousands of rare and endangered Asian plants and trees have been gathered from across the planet to be preserved and propagated in the Sonoma Valley. For more than three decades, Sonoma Botanical Garden has sheltered one of the largest collections of scientifically documented, wild-source, rare Asian plants and trees ever assembled.

The garden is a true horticultural ark, a defense against habitat loss, deforestation, climate change, agricultural expansion, and human consumption, which are all contributing to the near extinction of many "ancestor" species—those plants and trees from which the most popular species derive.

Lush and green in spring, dramatic in the winter, and blazing with color in summer and fall, the 67-acre garden is

## SONOMA BOTANICAL GARDEN

**WHAT:** A wander through a sanctuary for rare flora from around the world

**WHERE:** 12841 Hwy. 12, Glen Ellen

**COST:** Adults $12, seniors $10, children 13–17 $8, children 12 and under free

**PRO TIP:** If you're a rose fancier, notice the Chinese Heritage Rose Garden by the gift shop.

Of the more than 300,000 known species of plants, between 39% and 68% are threatened with extinction.

Top left: *This Japanese maple and dozens more throughout the Sonoma Botanical Garden burst into vivid oceans of color in the fall. Along the entry path into the garden, keep your eye out for the critically endangered, five-lobed maple,* acer pentaphyllum.

Top right: *Creeks, waterfalls, rivulets and fountains are among the delights in this horticultural haven.*

Bottom left: *Springtime blooming "Whitebark"* Magnolia obovate *is native to broadleaf forests in Japan. Ask about the* Magnolia sinica*, once logged for lumber; it's one of the most threatened magnolia species in the world, being propagated here in the garden.*

Bottom right: *Native to the Szechuan and Yunnan provinces in western China, the* Magnolia wilsonii *can grow to be 20 feet tall. Photos courtesy of the Sonoma Botanical Garden*

threaded with walking trails beloved by birders, photographers, and picnickers. To be discovered amid the flora are statuary, ponds, waterfalls, and wildlife. Ask about the location of what is said to be the rarest and most endangered maple in the world; with its spidery, deeply cut lobes, the *Acer pentaphyllum* has been duplicated here, and seed has been sent to its homeland in China, where it has died out. Also worth the find are the six *Magnolia sinica* here, among about only 50 in the world.

At the top of the garden where a string of Tibetan prayer flags flutter are views of Sonoma Mountain and the forested hills above Glen Ellen.

# NASCAR AND DRAGS

## What is Burnin' Bovine doing up there?

Wearing goggles and a helmet, with a live video screen, a large cow welcomes you from her perch on the Sonoma Raceway sign above Highway 37. Motorsports are on her bovine mind, as this race course rocks and rolls all year round with major events on the NASCAR circuit and the NHRA drag racing series. At the entrance to Sonoma Valley, the 2.52-mile, 12-turn, twisting, looping, hilly track is said to be one of the most challenging courses in the United States. For more than five decades, racing's biggest stars have been thrilling the crowds, including three-time Sonoma winner Martin Truex, and Kyle Busch, Tony Stewart, and five-time winner here, Jeff Gordon.

Special events such as the Ferrari Challenge, Superbike School, and Tough Mudder are more reasons to head for the raceway.

Amateur competitions and fundraisers give everyone a chance to hit the famous track. With a driver's license, you can compete in night drags, and screeching, smoking sideways

---

### SONOMA RACEWAY

**WHAT:** NASCAR, NHRA, and amateur racing and motorsports

**WHERE:** 29355 Arnold Dr., Sonoma

**COST:** From $10 for kids to $49–$180+ for adults

**PRO TIP:** Can't get to the races? Watch them on SonomaRaceway.com/live.

---

Drive your junker in "24 Hours of Lemons"! Pay $500 or less to see who survives, hissing and smoking and falling apart, in any street-legal vehicle with four wheels; no smog, insurance, or title required.

Top: *For ages 13 and up, open-wheel Go Karting on California's longest track. Photo courtesy of Sonoma Raceway*

Bottom left: *Professional stock car racing driver Martin Lee Truex Jr. is a three-time winner at Sonoma Raceway. Photo courtesy of Sonoma Raceway, N. Jacobson*

Bottom right: *Burnin' Bovine greets Sonoma Raceways fans as they head for NASCAR and NHRA events. Photo courtesy of Sonoma Raceway*

"drifting" races, which are wildly popular with spectators. "Laps for Charity" and "Hooked on Driving" programs also give amateurs a chance to hit the course in their own vehicles.

In June, the Sonoma Speed Festival recalls the golden days of racing when rare vintage vehicles hurtle around the track all weekend, and then parade to Sonoma Plaza for a car show. Go Karting and Kart Racing are electrifying, too, when drivers ages 13 and up careen around California's longest track at 70 miles per hour; don't worry, you can rent a kart, go to kart school, and practice.

# PLANT WIZARD'S GARDEN

## Who invented the spineless cactus and the plumcot?

In 1915, legendary inventors and entrepreneurs of their era, Henry Ford and Thomas Edison, rode in a private Northwestern Pacific railroad car from San Francisco Bay to Santa Rosa, where they were trailed by newspaper photographers and thousands of well-wishers to the home and experimental gardens of the most famous horticulturist on the planet, Luther Burbank. Today, you can make a pilgrimage to the world of the "plant wizard," where the three titans hobnobbed and Burbank showed off some of the 800 varieties of fruits, flowers, vegetables, and grains that he developed in the 1880s. He's known as the grandfather of the Russet potato, the Shasta daisy, and the spineless cactus, as well as myriad varieties of walnuts, almonds, plums, and apples.

## LUTHER BURBANK HOME AND GARDENS

**WHAT:** Home and gardens of a world-famous horticulturist

**WHERE:** 204 Santa Rosa Ave., Santa Rosa

**COST:** Free

**PRO TIP:** Although National Arbor Day is the last Friday in April, in California, Arbor Day is celebrated on March 7th, on Luther Burbank's birthday.

If you're hooked on horticulture, head over to Burbank's Gold Ridge Experiment Farm in Sebastopol to take a self-guided or docent-guided tour of his historic farm, cottage, and barn.

Top: *Beloved by the horticulturally inclined are the home and botanical gardens of the turn-of-the-century "plant wizard," Luther Burbank.*

Inset: *In 1915, Thomas Edison, Luther Burbank, and Henry Ford hobnob at Burbank's home and experimental gardens. Photos courtesy of Sonoma County Tourism*

Tucked away in a lush, tree-shaded botanical park in downtown Santa Rosa, Luther Burbank Home and Gardens promises a rewarding couple of hours exploring the garden guru's home, the carriage house museum, and the greenhouse and showplace gardens of this National Historic Landmark. Take a self-guided audio tour with a free trail map, or call ahead to book docent-guided explorations.

Along for the ride and the garden tour, rubber tire titan, Harvey Firestone, declared that Burbank was the "only man in this world who ever made botany as exciting as a horse race!"

# THE APPLE ABIDES

## When can we have the Grav?

In July and August, Sonomans are on the lookout for their favorite apple, the Gravenstein, available for just a few weeks, at you-pick farms, farmers markets, roadside stands, and grocery stores that carry local produce. Crisp, sweet, and tart, the Grav is unsurpassed for cooking and baking, juice, applesauce, cider, and brandy, and they were once shipped nationwide by the train car load. A major economic engine in the county for decades, in their heyday, Gravenstein apples, applesauce, and dried apples were shipped to US troops during World War II.

Modern hybrid varieties now stay fresher longer and can be machine harvested, resulting in the long, slow demise of the Grav as a "shipper." The only place in the world to get them now is Sonoma County, where a few growers remain, some harvesting from century-old trees. The history of the iconic apple is dappled. In the 17th century, Count Frederik the Younger is said to have discovered the variety at an Austrian monastery, while some historians believe the Spaniards brought it north into Alta California. In the early 1800s, the Russians at Fort Ross had Gravs in their vast orchards, and by mid-century, they were planted widely in the region.

Still Grav-crazy after all these years, Sebastopol regards itself as the Gravenstein capital of the world. During the annual Gravenstein Apple Fair there in August, a banner hangs over

Sebastopol's Apple Blossom Festival in April kicks off with a parade of marching bands, fruit growers' floats, school kids, and vintage farm equipment. Live music flows, as does cider, beer, and wine.

GRAVENSTEIN Apple Fair 2019

August 17th & 18th 10am - 6pm
RAGLE RANCH PARK  SEBASTOPOL, CALIFORNIA

*The iconic, historic Gravenstein apple is celebrated at the annual Gravenstein Apple Fair and throughout the county in July and August, when the apples are ripe. Pies ensue.*

Right: *Photo courtesy of Gravenstein Apple Fair, Mary Haffner*

Top left: *Photo courtesy of Gravenstein Apple Fair, Karen Pavone*

Bottom left: *Photo courtesy of Gravenstein Apple Fair, Jim Noonan*

## THE GRAVENSTEIN APPLE

**WHAT:** Recalling agricultural history, a heritage apple is celebrated at fairs, festivals, and parades.

**WHERE:** Sebastopol and around the county

**COST:** Free

**PRO TIP:** Mom's Apple Pie on the roadside near Sebastopol bakes Gravs into legendary homemade pies. "Mom" is Betty Carr, the one in the red-checked apron.

Sebastopol's main street announcing, "The Gravensteins are coming!" Pie making and apple juggling contests ensue, along with pig races, hayrides, and tastings of local cheeses, cider, and wine. Families learn how to build backyard earthen ovens and beehives, and other agrarian skills.

# JETS, COPTERS, PLANES

## Where can we see fighter jets?

Displaying nearly 40 rare, authentically restored military, propeller, and jet aircraft, the Pacific Coast Air Museum is located at the Charles M. Schulz Sonoma County Airport. You can crawl under the planes, explore wheel wells and bomb bays, and peer into the cockpits of World War II, Korea, Vietnam, and newer fighter jets.

You'll see an A-26 Invader attack bomber and an F-4C Phantom, an F-5E Tiger II, an F-14 Tomcat, a Huey helicopter, and many more planes. Besides the world's lightest jet aircraft, a historic aerobatic, bright-red Pitts Special; and components of the S-R 71 Blackbird spy plane, on view is the first responder F-15 Eagle, the first of the fighter planes dispatched over New York and Washington, DC, on 9/11. You can't miss the massive S-2A Tracker aerial firefighting tanker from the California Department of Forestry, and the C-18 Liftmaster used in the Korean conflict.

## PACIFIC COAST AIR MUSEUM

**WHAT:** Military planes from World War II, the Korea and Vietnam conflicts, and more restored vintage aircraft

**WHERE:** One Air Museum Way, Santa Rosa

**COST:** $10 adults, $7 seniors, $3 ages 6–17, free for 5 and under and military

**PRO TIP:** For a small fee, try out a 3D virtual reality flight simulator in a variety of aircraft, including a DC 10, a P-51 Mustang, and an F-18 Hornet.

The annual airshow, "Wings over Wine Country," has drawn more than 20,000 visitors to see jet demos, skydiving, hang gliding, aerobatics, and special tours.

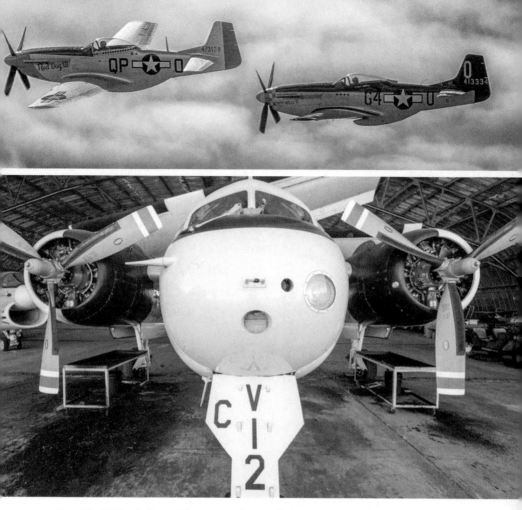

Top: *World War II, Korea, Vietnam, and newer fighter jets, helicopters, and other vintage planes are on display at the Sonoma County Airport, along with a museum of photos, models, souvenirs, and climb-in cockpits.*

Bottom: *An anti-submarine aircraft used by the US Navy, this Grumman S-2 Tracker air tanker now carries fire retardant for the California Department of Forestry and Fire Protection. Photos courtesy of Pacific Coast Air Museum*

An indoor museum displays artifacts, photos, models, videos, and climb-in cockpits. Adjacent to the outdoor museum, notice the airplane hangar, built during World War II, which was used in the 1963 movie *It's a Mad, Mad, Mad, Mad World*. In the movie, a Beech D-18 was flown at about 150 knots through the hangar with only 23 feet of clearance.

# RIDIN' A REAL TRAIN

## Where is that whistle blowing?

As the #1 attraction in the town of Sonoma for families of young children, TrainTown is a small, but mighty, amusement park. The main draws are the quarter-scale, open-air, bright-red railroad cars pulled by real steam and diesel locomotives and operated by conductors. A roundhouse with a turntable completes the authentic railroad backdrop.

Four miles of track meander, three times per ride, in 10 acres of lush Japanese-style garden and forest, through tunnels, past waterfalls and miniature gold rush–era buildings, and over bridges, to a stop at "Lakeview," a tiny Western town with a petting zoo. The "old" mill wheel actually turns in a running stream, and you can explore inside the little school, church, jail, and saloon; adults, duck your heads! The goats, ducks, llamas, chickens, sheep, and bunnies here are very tame and used to encounters with little ones.

A few blocks north on Broadway in the town plaza are two playgrounds, and picnic tables.

---

## SONOMA TRAINTOWN RAILROAD

**WHAT:** A kid-sized train, petting zoo, and amusement rides

**WHERE:** 20264 Broadway, Sonoma

**COST:** $7.50 per person, per train ride; $3.75 per person for other rides

**PRO TIP:** Adjacent to TrainTown is Jacob's Restaurant, a popular pizza place.

*The top family attraction in Sonoma, TrainTown sports a quarter-scale, open-air railroad pulled by real steam and diesel locomotives; destination: "Lakeview," a miniature Western town. Kids will also enjoy a carousel and kid-sized amusement rides. Top photo courtesy of TrainTown, inset photo courtesy of Sonoma County Tourism*

Back at the train station around a big pond are small-scale carnival rides, including the Locomotion Scrambler and a Mine Train coaster. The Air Scooter is a sweet little whirler of kids-only biplanes that "fly" around and around. A traditional, mirrored, pink-striped "High Iron" carousel is the glamorous centerpiece of the train park; the carousel and all the rides, except the planes, are sized for adults to accompany the kids.

You can also climb around in the train station; grab burgers, hot dogs, and ice cream at the snack bar; and pick up those irresistible train-related souvenirs.

# ON SAFARI IN SONOMA

## Is that a new gnu I see?

Founded in 1993 by an African antelope fancier who established his own conservation breeding facility, Safari West is a preserve for exotic African animals and birds that is open to the public and is entirely unlike a traditional zoo. In a strikingly beautiful grassland and forest setting northeast of Santa Rosa, it's a real bucket list destination—about as close as you can come to Africa and the Serengeti without being there. On day trips, visitors climb aboard authentic safari vehicles and slowly move around on three-hour guided tours to see nearly 1,000 animals, including 90 or so species from antelopes and gazelles to rhinos, cheetahs, giraffes, primates, zebras, buffalos, and a breathtaking array of birdlife.

## SAFARI WEST

**WHAT:** One of the premier wildlife preserves in the United States

**WHERE:** 3115 Porter Creek Rd., Santa Rosa

**COST:** Single day visits: adults $93–$128; ages 4–12 $45–$50; discounts for teens and seniors

**PRO TIP:** Nosh at the Savannah Café, with giraffes as your audience and a menu inspired by the South African braai (BBQ). You can dine indoors amid African artworks or on the veranda near the flamingo ponds and aviaries.

Book ahead for the "Winos and Rhinos" wine tasting, "Brews and Buffalo" beer tasting, and "Cheetahs and Chardonnay" dinners in the aviary.

*Giraffes and rhinos and zebras, oh my! More than 90 species of exotic African animals and birds live in a vast grassland and forest setting where visitors trundle through on authentic safari vehicles. Photos courtesy of Safari West*

The day tour also includes a walk to see the Amani Oasis Aviary, where cranes stalk about the footpath and scarlet ibis soar overhead. On view here are black-and-white colobus monkeys, cheetahs, and flamingos showing off their vivid plumage in the lagoon. New babies here are big news, when animal lovers get to suggest names for the newborns, such as Ollie and Oli, the giraffe calves, and Butternut and Taro, squealing Red River hoglets.

Lodging is available in luxurious, African-style tent cabins imported from Botswana, with private decks from where you can watch grazing antelope and listen to the sounds of the wild.

# A RAMBLING RANCHO

## Where is the largest original adobe building in the United States?

In 1834, when Alta California was under the control of the Mexican military, General Mariano Vallejo was awarded a vast land grant, including a hilltop for a hide and tallow factory. Today, you can visit his whopping-massive headquarters, preserved at Petaluma Adobe State Historic Park, on a country road between the towns of Sonoma and Petaluma.

The hub of Vallejo's 100-square-mile rancho between 1836 and 1846, which is a National Historic Landmark today, the Petaluma Adobe was constructed of handmade adobe brick and hand-hewn redwood hauled here by oxen from northern forests. Visitors can see how the adobe was held together with wooden nails, rawhide lashings of the beams, and a hand-split shingle roof. Park rangers and docents are on hand to explain the authentic artifacts and exhibits that portray life as it was in the on-site Native American village,

Docent-led tours are given on most weekends from 1 to 3 p.m.

*The heart of a 100-square-mile Mexican rancho between 1836 and 1846, a National Historic Landmark, life at the Petaluma Adobe is re-created at the annual Living History Day by costumed vaqueros, traders, soldiers, and Native American craftspeople. Photo courtesy of Petaluma Adobe State Historic Park*

including animal raising, agriculture, and daily work in the factory. About 2,000 indigenous people lived on the rancho, working at trades they learned at nearby Mission San Francisco Solano. They tended large herds of horses, sheep, and cattle; wove blankets and clothing; and became experts at blacksmithing. In the tannery, they produced leather for saddles, bridles, and other goods.

Outdoors are picnic sites, an entire fence of prickly pear cactus, and footpaths along Adobe Creek, shaded by oaks, willows, and buckeyes. Look for the nonindigenous species—the Australian bunya-bunya pine, the cork oaks, and the Chinese pistache trees.

# PLENTY OF PLINY

## Why do beer lovers from around the world come to Sonoma County in February?

If you love beer, you know about Pliny the Elder and Pliny the Younger. First brewed in 1995, one of the first commercially brewed double India Pale Ales (IPAs), the Elder was a smash hit from day one, and after years of limited availability and growing cult status, it's now on sale throughout the year.

A 21st-century phenom, the Younger is a triple IPA, meaning that it's higher in alcohol and has tons of hops, bitterness, and aromatics.

In the annual massing of beer geeks, hundreds of people stand in line for hours during the first two weekends in February at the Russian River Brewing Company brewpubs in Windsor and Santa Rosa to get just a glass or two and to purchase a couple of bottles to take home. Pliny the Younger sells out, period, and remains unavailable until the next year. In 2020, the pubs hosted more than 24,000 visitors who added $5 million to the local economy. And get this—local hotels offer special "Younger Rates" during the annual beer bedlam.

Besides on the February weekends, the Brewing Company's mothership is a fun tourist attraction in Windsor. The 85,000-square-foot facility comprises production, a brewpub, outdoor beer garden, gift shop, and tasting room; growler fills, and guided and self-guided tours are offered. If you're one

Said to be the first ever to refer to hops in writing, the first-century philosopher, Pliny the Elder, died in 79 AD while trying to save family and friends during the eruption of Mt. Vesuvius.

Left top and bottom: *Brewpubs in Santa Rosa and Windsor attract big crowds in February when artisan beers, Pliny the Elder and Pliny the Younger, are released. It's a Pliny cult! Photos courtesy of Russian River Brewing Company*

Right: *The Russian River Brewing Company in Windsor is open year-round for tours and beer-tasting on the patio. Photo courtesy of Sonoma County Tourism*

of the lucky ones, store your precious Older and Younger in the fridge and drink it soon, as the beer is brewed and delivered frequently, very fresh, to preserve that uber-hoppy flavor. And if the Pliny is all gone when you get to the head of the line, you can choose from a whole line of other yummy brews.

## THE CULT OF PLINY

**WHAT:** Follow the beer-lovin' crowd to Pliny the Elder and the Younger.

**WHERE:** 700 Mitchell Ln., Windsor; and 725 4th St., Santa Rosa

**COST:** Depends on what you are drinking or ordering to ship: about $60 for 12 bottles of the Elder

**PRO TIP:** Artisan beers and ciders are booming in Sonoma County. Seismic Brewing Company in The Barlow industrial park in Sebastopol pours sustainably crafted beers in a 4,000-square-foot taproom, while Golden State Cider serves vegan-friendly, gluten-free dry ciders.

# HAIL TO THE COUNT!

## Who was the "father of the California wine industry"?

A flamboyant and rather eccentric Hungarian Count, Agoston Haraszthy de Mokesa, fled his homeland, founded a town in Wisconsin, then led a wagon train to California in 1849 and was elected to the California State Assembly, ran the San Francisco Mint, and in 1857 founded Buena Vista Winery, California's first premium commercial winery. He kick-started the wine industry here with his planting of European varietals and through his travels around the world, where he proclaimed a glowing future for this new grape-growing region and gathered vine cuttings that were the foundation of the industry. Tucked away in a redwood forest on the outskirts of the town of Sonoma, Buena Vista Winery is today a landmark complex of magnificent stone buildings, the historic Press House, formal gardens, and leafy picnic sites.

### FATHER OF MODERN VITICULTURE IN CALIFORNIA

**WHAT:** A gregarious historic figure strides the halls of a California Historic Landmark winery.

**WHERE:** Buena Vista Winery, 18000 Old Winery Rd., Sonoma

**COST:** Free to see; fees for wine tasting and tours

**PRO TIP:** Haraszthy died as flamboyantly as he lived, in an alligator-infested river in the jungles of Nicaragua.

As "the Count," Webber presents a virtual series of cooking shows, *Cooking with the Count*, featuring sumptuous recipes paired with Buena Vista wines.

*George Webber as Count Agoston Haraszthy de Mokesa, the "Father of Modern Viticulture in California." Photos courtesy of George Webber*

When you visit, if you see a man in period costume and top hat spouting stories of the early days of wine making, you're looking at actor George Webber, who impersonates the Count at special events and in his booming voice narrates tours of the winery's impressive Wine Tool Museum. From time to time at events in town, he also becomes Mark Twain and General Mariano Vallejo.

# PEDAL YOUR TROLLEY

## How do you have a party on a bike?

The charming Victorian town of Healdsburg just begs for a unique way for visitors to sightsee and wine taste in style around the plaza and the tree-shaded streets. Turning heads when it rolls through town is the bright red party bike from Bike Healdsburg. Up to a dozen merrymakers can climb onboard and belly up to the bar, and everyone pedals to keep the mobile party moving.

You and your family and friends can sign on for an exercise tour, an architecture exploration, or the most popular expeditions that stop at three wineries and glide by historic sights. You can also choose a bar or brew crawl, or even a progressive dinner at several restaurants, which, in this town, is on every foodie's bucket list.

### PARTY BIKES IN HEALDSBURG

**WHAT:** Sightseeing and wine tasting on a bicycle built for 13

**WHERE:** Healdsburg

**COST:** $119 per person for 6–9 people; $99 per person for 10–12 people

**PRO TIP:** Decorate the bike with your own balloons, streamers, and banners!

Representing many of the more than 60 wineries in the adjacent Dry Creek Valley are a plethora of wine-tasting salons located right around the downtown Healdsburg Plaza.

*See the historic sites of Healdsburg and pedal your way to wine-tasting adventures along with your friends and family aboard a bright red party bike. Photos courtesy of Bike Healdsburg*

The most popular adventure on the rolling party, "Wine Tasting and Nibbles," lasts three hours, for art gallery visits and guided tastings at three wineries and a local vodka distillery (one of their specialties is H.O.B.S., or Harbor of Broken Souls).

Getting the group's heart rates up, the exercise tour is an hour meandering through downtown and across the Healdsburg Memorial Bridge over the river and back, while the history and architecture tour hits historic sites and makes a stop at the Healdsburg Museum.

# SEALS AND SEA STACKS

## Why are there so many seals in one place?

One of the most photogenic and prominent geological monuments on the North Coast, Goat Rock crouches like a lion at the mouth of the Russian River, which empties into the Pacific right here. Along with hundreds of other vertical columns of rock that you can see from here and that characterize the entire uniquely rugged northern California coastline, Goat Rock is a sea stack, a dramatic vestige of 20 to 30 million years ago when the continental plates collided, creating pillars still visible today. In the summertime, a sandbar appears along the beach, creating a lagoon separating the river from the ocean, and that becomes the temporary home of a large colony of harbor seals, and occasionally sea lions and even fur seals, who birth, nurse, and shelter their pups from predators between March and August. The flip-flopping seals along the edge of the sandbar

### GOAT ROCK

**WHAT:** A geological landmark and marine life gathering place

**WHERE:** Hwy. 1 and Goat Rock Rd., Jenner

**COST:** Free

**PRO TIP:** Watch for the hang gliders who launch from a 150-foot-high bluff above the south end of the beach.

Just south of Goat Rock Beach, look in the rocky outcrops above the shoreline to see smooth, glossy areas, signs that Ice Age mammoths rubbed their coats here about 12,000 years ago.

*Seals and sea lions frolic and shelter their pups at the mouth of the Russian River at Goat Rock, one of the most monumental "sea stacks" of many along the Sonoma Coast. Goat Rock Beach is a favorite whale-watching and driftwood gathering spot. Photo courtesy of Sonoma County Tourism*

are the males, protecting their families. Keep your eyes peeled for river otters in the warm waters of the lagoon.

From the driftwoody beach, you may well see whales during their migration season, November through April. The presence of the harbor seals makes this a popular stopping point for the whales on their round-trip from Alaska to Baja.

# TRAINS, TEAPOTS, RODEOS

## Where did all the railroads go?

Just four miles from the Pacific Coast, in the last half of the 20th century, Duncans Mills was a logging and sawmill settlement from where redwood was shipped by narrow-gauge railroad to the burgeoning big city by the bay. Today, the only remaining North Pacific Gauge Railroad station is a museum, here, displaying historic photographs, memorabilia, and old rail cars. In the 1870s, when the railroad reached all the way from the San Francisco Bay to rustic vacation resorts along the Russian River, Duncans Mills was a popular destination, which it still is today. The resident population is about the same as a century ago, less than 200.

Fishing is fabulous here near the steel bridge, for shad and catfish in the spring, bass in the summer, and Chinook salmon and steelhead in the wintertime. A campground popular with fishermen and families lies on the riverside.

In a rampant, overgrown garden setting, locals chit chat in restored clapboard buildings in their galleries, cafes, and antique and curio shops. In a museum-like atmosphere, Christopher Queen Galleries showcases early California landscape paintings, depicting pristine forests, meadows, and farmlands from the 1860s to the 1940s. The tea shop sells 100

## DUNCANS MILLS

**WHAT:** A museum-like, old loggers' village on the way to the coast

**WHERE:** Hwy. 116 and Moscow Rd.

**COST:** Breakfast and lunch start at $8.25, dinner at $17.50.

**PRO TIP:** The Old Spanish Days Fiesta, a nearly 100-year tradition, takes place every August with parades, rodeos, and live music.

Left inset and right inset: *A logging settlement in the 1800s, Duncans Mills is a charming collection of historic buildings housing galleries, eateries, and antiques and curio shops. On the way to the nearby coast, daytrippers stop at the general store for picnic provisions.*

Bottom: *At Duncans Mills, the circa-1870 North Pacific Gauge Railroad station is a museum today, displaying historic photographs, memorabilia, and old rail cars.*

exotic teas and fanciful teapots, Sophie Cellars pours wine on the patio, Cape Fear Café offers local seafood with a Southern flair, and the general store is the place for picnic provisions.

On Hwy. 116, watch for the sign to Villa Grande, a riverbend community in a 1920s time warp with undiscovered beaches and delightful lanes of early California craftsman-style cottages.

# A WHALE OF A TIME

## Is that the Loch Ness monster or a whale?

What are those water spouts in the ocean? When you see 15-foot-high water spouts along the Sonoma coastline, you're whale-watching! Sonoma County's coastal bluffs are perfect perches from which to spot whales cruising along, stopping to feed, and playing around during their annual migrations from November through April. Gray, blue, and humpback whales make their way from the Arctic, Alaska, and environs, heading south to give birth in the warm lagoons and bays of Baja California. On their way back north in the spring, babies are commonly seen swimming close to their mothers. With binoculars, you may also see dolphins, seals, and even orcas, which are now spotted far south of their natural habitat.

Among the best whale-watching spots is Bodega Head, near the West Trail parking lot. Here, Stewards of the Coast and Redwoods volunteers

---

## BEST PLACES TO WHALE WATCH

**WHAT:** Best spots on the Sonoma coast for whale-watching

**WHERE:** Seaside blufftops between Bodega Bay and The Sea Ranch

**COST:** Free

**PRO TIP:** Whale-watching cruises are offered from seaside communities, the Bodega Bay Sport Fishing Center, North Bay Charters, and others.

---

The gray whale can be 60 feet long and weigh more than 90,000 pounds, living as long as 70 years; the largest creatures thought ever to exist, blue whales can be 100+ feet long.

*On Sonoma County's coastal bluffs, November through April, you can spot whales cruising along, stopping to feed, and playing around during their annual migrations from the Arctic and Alaska to Baja California, and back. Top photo courtesy of Sonoma County Regional Parks, bottom left photo courtesy of Sonoma County Tourism*

with scopes and binoculars are often on hand to help visitors spot whales, and they explain the migration and natural history. Other good viewing locations are Timber Cove, Fort Ross, Sea Ranch, Gualala Point, Stillwater Cove Regional Park, and Salt Point State Park. Along their way up and down the California coastline, whales stop to feed in San Francisco Bay, in the Farallones, at Half Moon Bay and Point Reyes, and parts south.

# WALLS WITH STORIES

## Who are those larger-than-life-sized women?

Depicting three women activists who work on behalf of social justice, Black Lives Matter, and indigenous peoples' issues, the *Trinity Mural* emblazons the side of 3 Disciples Brewing pub in Santa Rosa. The flamboyant, building-sized masterpiece is just one of an impressive array of outdoor public art throughout the county. A tour of the city turns up more vibrant murals on the Roxie Theater and in Juilliard Park, plus whimsical installations up 4th Street and around the main plaza on planter boxes, fences, parking garages, and as freestanding sculptures. Art-loving explorers will find the online map handy as it locates nearly 60 works in downtown Santa Rosa alone.

The winner of a judged competition for a visual landmark at the intersection of five streets, Boback Emod's *Wholesome* towers over traffic with a steel ring supported by a massive, rust-hued arch. In addition, across the entire front of the Backstreet Studios Gallery building in "Art Alley" is a striking representation of Picasso's iconic *Guernica*.

In the town of Windsor at the Cali Calmecac language academy, local artists and students created a multicolored mural of Latino heritage and culture. Stretching 60 feet across the side of the Republic of Thrift shop in Sonoma's Boyes Hot Springs neighborhood, the 15-by-60-foot mural, *Vida de la Muerte*, was also painted by students, funded by an NEA grant, and overseen by world-famous spray paint artist, Chor Boogie.

More than 30 art studios and galleries in the South A Street (SOFA) arts district in Santa Rosa are open to the public during every "First Fridays Art Walk."

## CULTURAL MURALS AND ART ALFRESCO

**WHAT:** Exciting outdoor displays of public art around the county

**WHERE:** Vibrant murals and public art are found in nearly every Sonoma County town.

**COST:** Free

**PRO TIP:** After browsing the exhibits at the Petaluma Art Center, stop in next door at the Petaluma Visitors Center for a map of galleries and street art.

Top: *The building-sized* Trinity Mural *in Santa Rosa represents three local women activists who work for social justice, Black Lives Matter, and indigenous peoples' issues.*

Inset: *One of many murals and outdoor art installations in Sonoma County, Bud Snow's 62-foot-tall, 25-foot-wide mural emblazons the side of the Roxie Theater in Santa Rosa. Photo courtesy of Visit Santa Rosa*

In an old railroad depot, the heart and soul of Petaluma's lively art community, the Petaluma Art Center, is surrounded by outdoor art installations. A few blocks away, Ricky Watts's sinuous, dazzlingly bright 3,000-square-foot mural has transformed a wall of the century-old Phoenix Theater.

# VICTORIAN BEAUTIES

## Isn't that Pollyanna?

Although many Victorian mansions in Santa Rosa were lost in the 1906 earthquake, numerous impressive homes of the 1800s survived and are lined up on tree-shaded streets in a Historic District all their own. In those days, gables and pillars, turrets and porches, and fancy gingerbread trim were signs of wealth and importance, as they are today. A landmark among landmarks in the district, at 1015 McDonald Ave., "Mableton" was built circa-1879 with enough corbels, rosettes, balusters, spandrels, and general gewgaws to be the setting for Disney's 1960 movie, *Pollyanna*.

On the National Register of Historic Places, Mableton is a rare Stick-Eastlake style, a transition between Gothic Revival and Queen Anne, with an encompassing, columned veranda, tall gables, and floor-to-ceiling windows. At 14,000 square feet, Mableton is said to be the largest remaining structure of this specific style in existence. Today's "stickwork" exterior resembling Tudor half-timbering, and the richly decorated interior, are similar to the original, as in the 21st century, the house underwent a complete, authentic restoration.

Other neighborhood Victorians were in the movies, too, such as Alfred Hitchcock's *Shadow of a Doubt* at the oldest house in the district at 904 McDonald Avenue; the

## HISTORIC VICTORIAN ARCHITECTURE

**WHAT:** Architectural treasures in the Victorian historic district

**WHERE:** McDonald Ave., bounded by Fourth St., North St., and Bryden Ln., Santa Rosa

**COST:** Free

**PRO TIP:** Downtown, *Ca'Bianca* is a circa-1876 wedding-cake-white Victorian with a wraparound veranda, crystal chandeliers, stained glass, and antiques, comprising a sumptuous setting for an upscale restaurant.

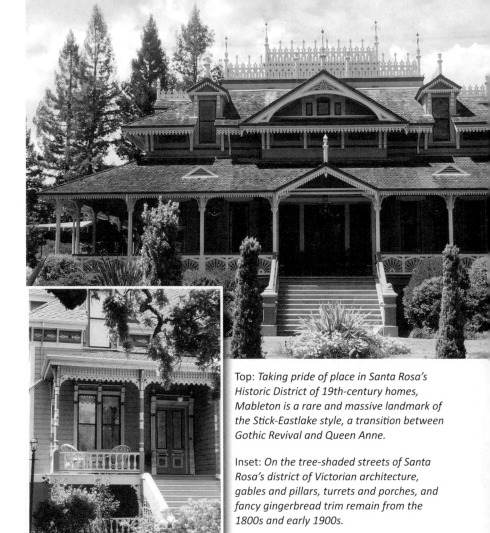

Top: *Taking pride of place in Santa Rosa's Historic District of 19th-century homes, Mableton is a rare and massive landmark of the Stick-Eastlake style, a transition between Gothic Revival and Queen Anne.*

Inset: *On the tree-shaded streets of Santa Rosa's district of Victorian architecture, gables and pillars, turrets and porches, and fancy gingerbread trim remain from the 1800s and early 1900s.*

thriller, *Scream*, at 815 McDonald; and the Burt Lancaster film, *All My Sons*, at 824 McDonald. On surrounding streets is an array of classic period styles from Tudor to Italianate, Gothic and Romanesque Revival, and some grand California craftsman homes from the early 1900s.

A gala Halloween "Fright Night" takes place in the historic district, with zombies, ghosts, and scaries handing out treats.

# DINOS, RHINOS, AND BEARS

## What's that dragon doing in my garden?

Driving along Highway 12 through Kenwood, it's impossible to miss Swede's Feeds, a one-of-a-kind plant nursery and outdoor art emporium that qualifies as a tourist attraction. A welded-metal menagerie of life-sized, captive animals looms menacingly by the roadside, from 12-foot-tall dinosaurs and giraffes to elephants, Bigfoot, skeletons, rearing horses, mammoths, and more. There are elaborate, multistory birdhouses and a line of recycled redwood boxes for bats and owls, plus, a family of flamboyantly pink, aluminum flamingos along with brightly hued peacocks, rustic roosters, black crows, giant bugs, and more yard art critters created from recycled tin drums, wine barrels, old machinery gears, and whatnot. You'll also find for sale chimineas (outdoor fire features), local honey, and fresh eggs.

Swede's is a certified Monarch Waystation, where the iconic orange and black butterflies flock to milkweed in the roadside garden. Headed for extinction, the Monarch is at about 1% of its historic population.

GARDEN SUPPLIES

ANIC LIZERS

WILD SUPPLI

*A rusted metal menagerie of captive exotic animals menace the roadside, from towering dinosaurs and giraffes to elephants and Bigfoot, skeletons, rearing horses, and mammoths, plus real wildlife and lots of garden plants.*

Kids love the live animals—pygmy goats, a flock of fancy chickens, rabbits, a frog and fish pond, Jazz the cat, and Chloe the white Lab.

Beyond the excitement of the eye-popping cross between Jurassic Park and Old MacDonald's farm is an open-air nursery specializing in non-GMO, organically grown home garden plants; wildly colorful ceramic pottery; and patio furniture built of wine barrel staves and recycled redwood chicken coops. You can get feed for your pot-bellied pig, hamster, pigeon, and canary here too.

# THE TSAR LOVED SONOMA

## Who were the first settlers in Sonoma County?

No, it wasn't the Spanish. In 1812, joining the indigenous Kashia Pomo people living in the area, Russian hunters, traders, and farmers were the first settlers on the coast, establishing the southernmost outpost of the Russian Empire in America, high on a bluff above the Pacific. Accompanied by native Alaskan Aleuts, they harvested sea otter and seal pelts, and grew produce for the Empire's more northerly camps. The whole shebang was protected by high bastions and a bristling line of cannons, just in case the Spanish decided to pay a call.

When the Mexican government and American settlers began to muscle in on the fur trade and threaten the Russians, they hightailed it back to the mother country in 1841. Today, Fort Ross State Historic Park creates a living

## FORT ROSS STATE HISTORIC PARK

**WHAT:** A restored encampment built by the Russians in the early 17th century

**WHERE:** 19005 Coast Hwy., 11 miles north of Jenner

**COST:** Day use fee $8 per vehicle

**PRO TIP:** Peer offshore to see sea lions and harbor seals lounging on Sea Lion Rocks; right below, Sandy Beach Cove is a small, protected beach with tide pools.

Kashaya Pomo called the Alaskan natives "underwater people" because their low-riding kayaks (*iqyans*) appeared to be emerging from the sea. The Alaskans paddled to the Farallon Islands and beyond, across the rough open ocean, where they hunted for months at a time.

*In the early 1800s, Russian sea otter and seal hunters, traders, and farmers were the first settlers on what is now the Sonoma Coast. Along with a contingent of indigenous tribal people, they established the southernmost outpost of the Russian Empire in America, high on a bluff above the Pacific. Top photo courtesy of Visit California, inset photo courtesy of Sonoma County Tourism*

history experience for visitors, who wander the grassy encampment and the restored and reconstructed redwood log structures—a stockade, a jewel of a Russian Orthodox chapel, barracks, a windmill, and the impressive Rotchev House, the only surviving Russian-built structure outside of Alaska.

In the visitor's center and throughout the settlement, you can see rifles, pistols, tools, furnishings, old photos, history exhibits, and films, as well as purchase guidebooks and even Russian chocolates. On the first Saturday of each month, demonstrations and guided tours are offered. Annual events and festivals feature history reenactments and Native American dancing.

# HERE COME THE BIRDS

## Are the birds gonna eat us, Mommy?

From the harbor side of the Tides Wharf Restaurant in Bodega Bay, if you've seen Alfred Hitchcock's movie *The Birds*, you'll recognize the road where Tippi Hedren drove her Aston Martin around the bay to get to Rod Taylor's house; here also is the dock where she rented the motorboat. This little New England–style fishing village and surroundings comprised the settings for Hitchcock's hair-raising, 1963 horror film about flocks of blackbirds and gulls attacking townspeople, swooping down on children, and pecking Hedren nearly to death. Hundreds of gulls, ravens, and crows were trained for the film, while mechanical birds and animations were used in some scenes.

The Tides is where Hedren, her love interest, Taylor, and the nervous locals gossiped, disagreed, panicked, and then hid from the birds in their boarded-up houses. Today, the sprawling seafood restaurant remains the heart of the town and a popular tourist attraction for seafood, bay views, and free entertainment by harbor seals and the comings and goings of fishing boats and sailing craft.

Just east of town above the Bodega Highway, the century-old Potter School was the site of the shocking scene where menacing black birds roosted by the hundreds on the playground equipment and attacked the kids, who ran screaming in terror down the street. Their teacher, Annie (who also hankered after

---

Hitchcock was said to have based *The Birds* on an incident in 1961 when flocks of dying birds poisoned by toxic plankton dropped out of the sky and flew into the windows around the city of Monterey.

Top: *Tippi Hedren starred in Alfred Hitchcock's 1963 thriller* The Birds, *which was filmed in and around Bodega Bay, including the fishing docks and The Tides, still a popular seafood restaurant today. Photo courtesy of The Tides, Bill Dow*

Middle: *The 1873 Potter School where menacing black birds roosted on the playground equipment before attacking the kids. Photo courtesy of The Tides*

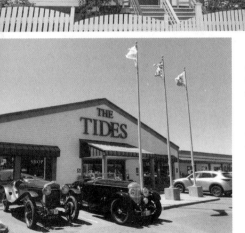

Bottom: *Today, the Tides restaurant in Bodega Bay made famous in* The Birds *is crowded with safe and happy diners. Photo courtesy of The Tides, Christian Galazzo*

Rod), played by Suzanne Pleshette, saved the children, but then was killed by the birds when she stepped outside. As Taylor drives out of town to take the injured Hedren to a hospital, birds are perched menacingly on tree branches, and reports of bird attacks in Santa Rosa play on his car radio.

# NATURE'S AQUARIUMS

## What's that nibbling on my toes?

Kids love nothing better than to explore tide pools when the tide is out so they can see and touch strange and magical creatures. The craggy, rocky Sonoma coastline is famous for its many tide pools, most of which are easily accessible along the 17-mile Sonoma Coast State Park from Bodega Bay to north of Jenner and beyond. Natural aquariums swaying with shallow seawater and kelp, the rocky basins are alive with hermit crabs, vivid starfish, flower-like anemones, purple urchins, mussels, and limpets, with miniature sculpin fish darting around. What could be more exciting and more educational than peering into such a colorful ecosystem?

A top site for tide pooling is Salt Point State Park, about 18 miles north of Jenner. Here at the Gerstle Cove Marine Reserve, you can scramble around in the pools, and you may also see scuba divers, harbor seals, and, in the wintertime, whales. The people in bright yellow or orange gear are marine scientists monitoring the seaweed, biodiversity, and invertebrates in the intertidal zone. Just above the cove, the visitors center sometimes offers guided tide pool tours.

Three miles south of Jenner, Shell Beach is a long, rocky and sandy stretch with tide pools so rich with marine life that school groups are commonly seen here. In spring and

---

### TIDE POOLS ON THE SONOMA COAST

**WHAT:** Tide pools rich with living marine creatures on a 17-mile stretch of beaches

**WHERE:** Sonoma Coast State Park, 3095 CA-1, Bodega Bay tide pool

**COST:** Free

**PRO TIP:** Best time of day is low tide when the pools are shallow, and there is less risk of wave action. Remember, live creature collecting is not allowed.

Top: *Kids never forget their explorations of Sonoma Coast tide pools, where at low tide, the rocky basins are alive with sea creatures. Photo courtesy of Bodega Marine Laboratory*

Inset: *Along with hermit crabs, starfish, purple urchins, mussels, and limpets, flower-like anemones can be found in the sea life-rich tidepools along the beaches of Sonoma Coast State Park. Photo courtesy of Sonoma County Tourism*

summer, you also may encounter roving naturalists who love to tell you all about what you're seeing. There's good fishing here too. Near Bodega Bay, crabs and other crustaceans are alive and well at Schoolhouse Beach, along with masses of starfish. Plan to wear shoes on the rocky beach here.

From Bodega Head to well north of Jenner, all along the Sonoma Coast, are parking spots on the clifftops with pathways leading down to beaches and tide pool areas.

# REDWOODS AND RAVIOLI

## Where can we go back in time and eat spaghetti?

In the late 19th century, the last stop west on the narrow-gauge North Pacific Coast Railroad was the logging encampment of Occidental, isolated up in dense redwood forests. In its heyday, lumber from six sawmills was trundled down the rails to Sausalito and ferried across the bay to San Francisco. When lodgings were built in the 1890s, vacationers rode the train up to Occidental to bask in the sunshine in a "well-built" town with "a neat depot, two shoemaker shops, four hotels, a winery, warehouses and commodious dwellings."

Today, the two-block-long main street is lined with original and re-created buildings from that era, housing restaurants, art galleries, and curio shops, plus two Italian restaurants that bring diners here from miles away—all great reasons to drive up the scenic Bohemian Highway to Occidental. For decades, these two pasta palaces have been family favorites for bountiful Italian dinners. A

## OLD OCCIDENTAL

**WHAT:** A weekend destination with history, art, and Italian food

**WHERE:** On the scenic Bohemian Highway, 9+ miles from Sebastopol

**COST:** Free

**PRO TIP:** In April, artists, musicians, and denizens of the town dress up, act silly, and carouse along in the annual Fool's Day Parade. Music, food, and high jinks ensue as well.

Bicyclers and motorcyclists ride right through town to corkscrew Coleman Valley Road, heading west all the way to Coleman Beach at the coast.

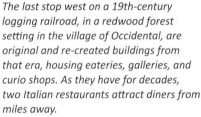

*The last stop west on a 19th-century logging railroad, in a redwood forest setting in the village of Occidental, are original and re-created buildings from that era, housing eateries, galleries, and curio shops. As they have for decades, two Italian restaurants attract diners from miles away.*

boarding house and saloon for railroad workers in the 1880s, the Union Hotel Restaurant is now a traditional Italian eatery, watering hole, and pizzeria with red-checked tablecloths and a wisteria-draped garden patio. Not to be outdone, Negri's Italian Dinners features made-from-scratch family recipes passed down four generations, such as Nonni's ravioli and cacciatore, as well as famous apple fritters.

A thriving colony of artists and craftspeople have their headquarters at Occidental Center for the Arts, where musical events and festivals are held each year. Local artists are also well represented at Hand Goods, a rambling emporium of art and crafts, such as pottery, jewelry, sculptures, textiles, prints, and clothing.

# GLAMPING IN STYLE

## Got ants in your pants and sand in your sleeping bag?

Do you dream of camping out without having to load the car, haul a trailer, or pitch a tent in the middle of the night? With the comforts of home and the amenities of luxury hotels, a new way to camp without roughing it is called glamping. You'll find glamping resorts all over Sonoma County, in forests and wildlife preserves, on blufftop retreats, and in secluded hideaways.

## CAMPING THE EASY WAY

**WHAT:** Glamping is camping with style and comfort.

**WHERE:** Near outdoor recreation, wineries, and historic sites in Sonoma County

**COST:** About $175 to $285 per night during the peak season

**PRO TIP:** Bring flashlights and/or lanterns, as some glampground accommodations are not electrified.

Nearby the town of Sonoma in the wooded foothills, hidden away in historic Westerbeke Ranch are tipi-like "Bell Tents," inviting retreats with duvet-covered beds and glowing lanterns, along with a nice bathhouse, a huge pool, and a hot tub.

East of Windsor, Safari West is a world-famous, 400-acre wildlife preserve that shelters and breeds African plains animals, which roam free. Plush, permanent tents here have viewing decks, en suite bathrooms, and ceiling fans. As an overnight guest, you may well hear the grunts of rhinos and the calls of the trumpeter hornbill, and the calls and rustlings of giraffes, zebras, antelopes, cheetahs, hyenas, and more.

At AutoCamp in the Russian River area, clustered in a Redwood grove are 24 sleek, "silver bullet" Airstream trailers sporting queen beds and sofa beds, TVs, kitchens, and showers. Guests gather in the moonlight around fire rings, reliving their adventures kayaking the Russian River or pedaling into Guerneville on the resort's cruiser bikes. A mid-century

Top left: *In a quiet corner of historic Westerbeke Ranch, tipi-like "Bell Tents" are inviting retreats. Photo courtesy of Westerbeke Ranch*

Top right: *Safari-style tent cabins in a world-famous preserve for African plains animals. Photo courtesy of Safari West*

Bottom left: *Near outdoor adventures to be had in the Russian River area in AutoCamp's Airstream trailers. Photo courtesy of Sonoma County Tourism*

Bottom right: *Glamping resorts are popping up all over Sonoma County. Photo courtesy of Visit California*

modern-style clubhouse and a firepit lounge enhance the glamping experience, and you can walk from here to a riverside beach, or drive into town for gallery browsing and restaurants. Just on the east side of Guerneville are the dramatic trees and walking trails of Armstrong Redwoods State Natural Reserve.

Glamping Hub is a booking agency for tents, cabins, campervans, yurts, tree houses, and other luxury camping accommodations.

# A MOOOVING EXPERIENCE

## Where can the family see farm animals up close?

Besides numerous dog parks in Sonoma County, you can also visit "cow parks." Cattle wander around on the 3,400 acres of grasslands of Tolay Lake Regional Park, in the verdant hills near Petaluma. Little kids love watching the big animals munch their way around the meadows. You might ask "Why are cows allowed in public parks?" They are here to help preserve the ecosystem by grazing down and fertilizing the native grasses, which then sprout fresh, new growth, all year round, rather than drying out and becoming fire hazards. Keeping your distance from the working animals and your dog on a leash, move slowly (and always close the gates behind you) to share the park safely with the livestock. Just don't try to pet those super-cute calves, as their moms may try to run you off.

Tolay is a favorite of bird-watchers, who head for the shallow freshwater lake, the creek, and the extensive wetlands, which are inhabited by waterfowl and more than 100 species of migrating and resident birds; golden eagles are spotted here too. On a dozen or so miles of trails on rolling hills, hikers, bikers, and horseback riders enjoy ridgetop views of San Francisco Bay and beyond.

At Taylor Mountain and Helen Putnam Regional Parks, you'll encounter very friendly and curious resident cows, and

The Federated Indians of Graton Rancheria demonstrate basket weaving, flint knapping, and other Native American skills at the Tolay Fall Festival.

*Visitors hiking, biking, and picnicking at some of Sonoma County's regional parks are surprised when they see cattle, sheep, and goats in the meadows and on the trails. Some of the cattle are residents, while sheep and goats, often in the hundreds, often "vacation" in a park for days at a time, grazing down and fertilizing the native grasses, which would otherwise become fire hazards.*

## COW PARKS

**WHAT:** Farm animal viewing, trail walking, bird-watching, biking, and hiking

**WHERE:** Tolay Lake Regional Park, 5869 Cannon Ln., Petaluma; Helen Putnam Regional Park, 411 Chileno Valley Rd., Petaluma

**COST:** $7 to park

**PRO TIP:** The annual two-weekend Tolay Fall Festival is all about a pumpkin patch, creepy creatures, hayrides, demos of astronomy, archery, and more.

sometimes you'll meet herds of hundreds of sheep and goats that are watched over by sheep dogs and shepherds. The cattle are residents, while the wooly weeders come and go, chomping away the weeds and the poison oak. At Putnam, six miles of walking trails meander over grassy hillsides and through oak woodlands; kids love the little fishing pond, the playground, and picnic grounds.

# SIZZZLING RETRO REGALIA

## Where can I get bell bottoms and a faux fur jacket for a 1970s party?

If you've ever worn a poodle skirt, cowboy boots, palazzo pants, or a smoking jacket, you'll be right back there at Hot Couture Vintage Fashion. In the Historic Railroad Square district since 1976, this is a vast emporium of fashion finds in clothing and accessories from the 1890s to the 1970s. Getting kitted out for costume parties, customers dress up in roaring 1920s beaded flapper dresses, mobsters' fedoras and zoot suits, fringed Elvis garb, and fruit-on-your-head Carmen Miranda outfits.

How about a kilt, designer jeans, or a feathered chapeau and a jeweled antique purse? For both men and women, the inventory is carefully purchased in perfect condition. Guys go for the aloha shirts and flared hippie pants

### HOT COUTURE VINTAGE FASHION

**WHAT:** The good old days of hot pants, gogo boots, and jean jackets at a beloved vintage clothing store

**WHERE:** 101 West 3rd St., Santa Rosa

**COST:** Free to see

**PRO TIP:** Also in Santa Rosa, Disguise the Limit is all about crazy costumes, horror masks, Gothic funk, and steampunk. Ask about the Haunted Couture Room, and don't miss a peek into the (empty) dressing rooms.

In a circa-1920 building in Cloverdale, more on the couturier side, Voss Signature Vintage specializes in glamorous attire from the 1920s on.

*Specializing in fashion finds from the 1890s to the 1970s, Hot Couture in the Historic Railroad Square district is a sprawling emporium of perfectly preserved clothing, costumes, and accessories. Try on a kilt, deck yourself out in a feather boa, pick up hippie garb or a wedding dress, and sashay away with a bejeweled handbag!*

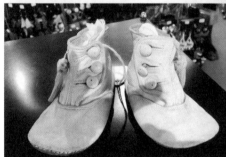

from the 1970s. And for all those rock concert T-shirts and college logo apparel, fur coats, and wedding gowns, fancy handbags and elbow-length gloves, now is the time to clear out your attic.

You can rent anything that you see at Hot Couture, and there is a large back-of-store area packed with costumes, from pirate garb to disco dresses and lederhosen, all completely accessorized with headgear, shoes, and jewelry.

# STONELACE AT THE SHORE

## Where can we see *tafoni*?

A strange and photogenic geological wonder is on abundant display above the six-mile-long, rocky shoreline at Salt Point State Park. Millions of years ago after the Ice Ages, the ocean receded, and sandstone formations from deep in the sea were tectonically uplifted into the marine terraces that you see today. Eons of salt then deposited and crystallized on the soft stone, transforming it into *tafoni* (the Italian word for "cavern"), which are hollows, cracks, knobs, and crevices that look like giant bees have built their vast honeycombs here. Near the shore, you'll see that limpets, sand crabs, and other creatures make their homes in the thousands of carved-out notches.

The remarkable "stonelace, swiss-cheese rock" formations are of fascination to geologists,

In the mid-1800s, sandstone blocks from Salt Point were cut and shipped to the new city of San Francisco for buildings and streets; you may spy eyebolts where ships tied in to be loaded.

*One of many geological oddities within Salt Point State Park is the miles-long stretch of tafoni, which are strange sandstone formations that have, over eons, pocked the marine terraces into honeycombs, hollows, cracks and knobs, as if a giant ice cream scoop has carved them out.*

student groups, and visitors who stop in at the Visitors Center for maps and information about the ancient formations. Call ahead to find out about guided tours and activities offered throughout the high season.

Along the six miles of rugged shoreline in the park are tide pools rich with marine life, plus an official underwater park, a pygmy forest, miles of trails, and a campground.

# HISTORY ON THE PLAZA

## Where is the largest original central plaza in California?

On the National Register of Historic Places, Sonoma's postcard-perfect town square is shaded by towering redwoods and firs, massive eucalyptus and graceful magnolias, creating idyllic picnic, playground, and festival venues. Ramble around the eight-acre plaza to see historic sites, such as a monument to the Raising of the Bear Flag here in 1846, marking the American revolt against Mexican rule. The commander of the local Mexican troops and the founder of the town, General Mariano Vallejo, today sits in bronze glory on a park bench, where tourists cozy up to him for selfies.

Anchoring a panoply of 19th-century buildings in and around the plaza is a Spanish Colonial Revival–style city hall and a Classical Revival–style former Carnegie Library that houses the Sonoma Valley Visitors Center. In a line-up of 200-year-old adobe buildings and Victorians are shops, eateries, and wine-tasting rooms. Founded in 1823, the Mission San Francisco de Solano holds pride of place here in the California State Historic Park, along with the barracks of the Mexican garrison.

Lively annual events take place in the plaza, from a nationally acclaimed, old-fashioned Fourth of July parade to a Cinco de Mayo festival, as well as Octoberfest, the Sonoma Plein Air Festival, a Mexican Independence Day celebration, wine festivals, and a wildly popular Farmers Market every Tuesday evening in the summertime, with live music, food trucks, and

---

The open-air Sonoma Valley Wine Trolley trundles wine enthusiasts and sightseers on a six-hour ride through Sonoma Valley from the plaza to wineries and includes a gourmet lunch.

**WHAT:** History, wining, dining, and celebrations around a tree-shaded plaza

**WHERE:** First Street East and Broadway, Sonoma

**COST:** Free, except for Sonoma State Historic Park buildings

**PRO TIP:** Surrounding the plaza are more than two dozen wine-tasting establishments.

Top left: *The historic heart of the largest original town plaza in California is Mission San Francisco de Solano.*

Top right: *Brilliant beauties at the annual Sonoma Speed Festival vintage car rally at the Sonoma City Hall in the plaza.*

Bottom left: *Topped by a soaring clock tower looming above the town plaza, the rosy pink, neon-flashed Sebastiani Theatre is a classic 1930s Italian Renaissance-style movie palace complete with vintage film memorabilia, one large screen on a stage that often sees live performances, and fancy, gold-painted embellishments. Photos courtesy of Sonoma Valley Visitors*

displays of locally grown produce. Thirsty history buffs end up at Plaza Bistro, where the oldest bar in town was shipped here around Cape Horn in 1874—even favorite son, the author Jack London, was said to belly up to the bar here.

# FLUTTERING IN THE WIND

## Where are kinetic sculptures in Sonoma County?

They flutter and sparkle, flow, and mist, coming alive in wind, light, fog, fire, and water. Ned Kahn's kinetic sculptures are seen around the county and the world. It may be the side of a high-rise building appearing to move in waves or water falling through a trembling grid.

On the edge of the roof at the Museum of Sonoma County, a long, white aluminum fence undulates and whispers constantly with every breath of air movement. Destined for the rooftop of the new Hotel Sebastopol, the 44 foot-long *Wind Hammock* undulates and glistens in the breeze, promising rest and reflection for hotel guests. A wall of 30,000 wind-animated panels sparkle across the west facade of the ATT Building in downtown Santa Rosa, while in a bucolic setting on the Junior College campus, 1,000+ translucent turbines in a tall grid spin gracefully in the wind.

## KINETIC SCULPTURES

**WHAT:** A collection of large-format, outdoor kinetic art on view throughout Sonoma County

**WHERE:** Above, and as noted on the artist's website

**COST:** Free

**PRO TIP:** Inspired by the Laguna Wetlands freshwater marsh in Sebastopol, plans are underway by the artist for a 60-foot-tall spire sculpture at the entrance to the town.

Ned Kahn was awarded a MacArthur Foundation Genius Grant in 2003.

Top left: *Against a leafy backdrop at Paradise Ridge Winery, Ned Kahn's* Encircled Cloud Mist *billows from a six-foot-diameter stainless steel ring. Photo courtesy of nedkahn.com*

Top right: *Across the roof of the Museum of Sonoma County, Ned Kahn's glittering, undulating fence catches the eye. Photo courtesy of the Museum of Sonoma County*

Bottom: *Among many of Ned Kahn's kinetic sculptures in Sonoma County,* Wind Hammock *glistens in the wind above quivering discs.*

At the entryway to H2 Hotel in Healdsburg, as part of the rain-gathering system of the building, Kahn created *Spoonfall* with 2,000 suspended espresso spoons activated by trickling water, filling and dipping and spilling into a continually changing pattern.

In the sculpture garden at Paradise Ridge Winery, one of the artist's many installations activated by mist or fog, *Encircled Cloud Mist* billows from a six-foot-diameter stainless steel ring, framing the leafy landscape beyond; visitors love to run through the refreshing ring.

# THE WATER WHEEL TURNS

## Where is the hall of history in Glen Ellen?

Watch for the giant water wheel in Glen Ellen at Jack London Village, where restaurants, a chocolate shop, wine tasting, an art gallery, and 19th-century history are reasons to stop. While here, if you don't happen to go looking for the restrooms, you will miss the Glen Ellen Historical Society's "History Center" in an obscure hallway. On view in vintage photos and memorabilia are the area's early wine making, and the audacious lives of novelist Jack London and his wife, Charmian, whose "Beauty Ranch," now a state park, is just up the hill.

In a leafy forest setting, the landmark waterwheel and rustic, redwood-sided buildings remain from when a redwood log sawmill operated here on the creek side in 1829, before it became a gristmill and a stagecoach stop, and later a winery and distillery, right through Prohibition. At the entrance to The Mill at Glen Ellen restaurant are the original millstones that were shipped around the Horn from France.

If you hang out at the bar here, try to imagine when Jack London rode his horse down from the ranch and threw back a few with his poker-playing cronies. London would have

Just up the road from here is Jack London State Historic Park. Stop first at Glen Ellen Village Market for gourmet picnic provisions and wine to be enjoyed in the park or at tables behind the market.

Right: *On the creek side at Jack London Village, a giant water wheel remains from an 1800s redwood log sawmill.*

Inset: *Waiting to be discovered in a hallway at Jack London Village, a display of vintage photos and documents traces Sonoma Valley's early wine making and the adventurous life of author Jack London.*

## HIDDEN HALL OF HISTORY

**WHAT:** On a country road, history, food and wine, and an art walk

**WHERE:** 14301 Arnold Dr., Glen Ellen

**COST:** Free to see

**PRO TIP:** On the porch, pluck a book from the free library shelves, and when you have a chance, contribute one.

loved the place today, where wood-fired pizza, steaks, and seafood are paired with house-brewed beer and local wines.

Dramatic art pieces stand throughout the sprawling, tree-shaded property, from large spheres and shifting kinetic pieces to intriguing ceramic figures. The intricate, suspended *Yellow Disk* and the soaring steel and titanium *Iketo Yama* are eye-catching works, along with a provocative woman, *Listening for Sounds of Joy*, just below the deck at Yeti Restaurant, which specializes in East Indian and Nepalese food.

# EARLY CALIFORNIA HISTORY

## Are all the California missions in one place?

The California Missions Museum offers a rare opportunity to "see" and learn about all 21 California missions. Along El Camino Real, from San Diego to Sonoma, they were built by Spanish Franciscan missionaries as frontier outposts, between 1769 and 1823. Tucked in a garden setting behind the Cline Family Cellars winery in the Sonoma Valley, the museum displays small-scale models of all the missions as they were created for the 1939 California Exposition in San Francisco. The Cline Family saved the models from being auctioned off individually and, in 2005, designed and built the museum just for these historical treasures.

If you have a fourth-grader, this is a must; each year, 4,000 grade school students visit the museum as part of their California history curriculum. Each in

### CALIFORNIA MISSIONS MUSEUM

**WHAT:** The 21 California missions in a historical display

**WHERE:** Cline Family Cellars, 24737 Arnold Dr./Hwy. 121, Sonoma

**COST:** Free

**PRO TIP:** On the winery grounds, look for a small chapel topped by a bell and constructed with 1,200 handmade adobe bricks from original Mission San Francisco Solano.

Mission construction came to an end in 1823 in the town of Sonoma, where Mission San Francisco Solano is the last and northernmost of the California missions.

*In a winery estate in the Sonoma Valley, all 21 California missions are on view in small-scale models. Photo courtesy of Cline Family Cellars*

a clear acrylic box, the models are at eye level for most kids, and they are made of wood, clay, glass, cast iron, and plant material, detailed down to the shrubbery and tiny figures. The museum also includes a life-size figure of Father Junipero Serra, who gets the credit for establishing the missions; paintings of each mission; and striking stained-glass panels that were in Mission Dolores prior to the 1906 earthquake. History savvy docents are on hand to enhance visitor experience. The lush, rambling gardens and picnic areas make this a pleasant rest stop and wine-tasting opportunity.

**MILITARIA ON PARADE** (page 164)

**STARSTRUCK AT SUGARLOAF** (page 10)
Photo courtesy of Robert Ferguson Observatory

**CORK-POPPING HISTORY** (page 178)
Photo courtesy of Korbel Champagne Cellars

**HANGING OUT WITH *PEANUTS*** (page 18)
Photo courtesy of Charles Schulz Museum

**GIANT REDWOODS** (page 122)

**FLYING IN THE TREETOPS** (page 22)
Photo courtesy of Sonoma Canopy Tours

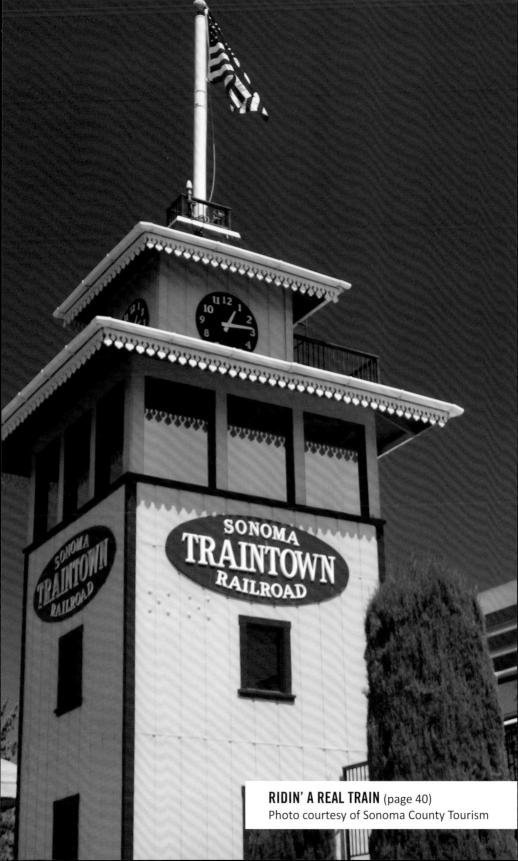

**RIDIN' A REAL TRAIN** (page 40)
Photo courtesy of Sonoma County Tourism

**JAPANESE-STYLE SERENITY** (page 148)
Photo courtesy of Osmosis Sanctuary

**CROSSING THE ART SPECTRUM** (page 174)

**WIND BENEATH YOUR WINGS** (page 2)

**A GHOSTLY FOREST** (page 8)

**ON SAFARI IN SONOMA** (page 42)
Photos courtesy of Safari West

**ART IN PARADISE** (page 168)

STONELACE AT THE SHORE (page 78)

**A PLEA FOR PEACE** (page 108)
Photo courtesy of Timber Cove Inn

**RUSSIAN TOTEMS** (page 110)
Photo courtesy of the Gualala Art Center

# FOOD TRUCKS, LATINO STYLE

## What does "mitote" mean?

An ancient Nahuatl word meaning "a festive gathering," *mitote* is all about food and fun at Mitote Food Park, the first Mexican food park in Northern California. Set up in the Roseland Village westside district of Santa Rosa are several gourmet food trucks and the El Mercadito Farmers Market, which together create a grand celebration of the county's vibrant Latino culture, music, arts, and legendary street food.

Known for seafood, Rodrigo Mendoza runs El Charro Negro, where he serves up "beach and barrio" tacos, tostadas, and *aguachiles* filled with fresh shrimp, fish, calamari, oysters, and octopus. Mayan-style tamales and homemade mole sauces are on offer at the mobile kitchen, Aguachiles de Camarón, where lime-marinated shrimp ceviche is popular. At the bright-orange Lucha Sabina truck, it's authentic Oaxacan *comida* (main meal of the day) with a focus on mushrooms and *tlayuda* (Mexican pizza), barbacoa, *lengua* (beef tongue), chorizo, *tripas* (chitterlings), carnitas, asada, and *al pastor* (grilled pork taco).

---

This county is loaded with food trucks, from Tacos La Bamba at an auto repair shop in Boyes Hot Springs, to El Roy's Mexican Grill in Petaluma, famous for shrimp tacos and *horchata* (rice-based) drinks. Keep an eye out for Streetside Asian Grill for teriyaki bowls, spring rolls, and crab puffs.

*In the first Mexican food park in Northern California, brightly painted food trucks and El Mercadito Farmers Market create a vibrant Latino culture and cuisine destination in western Santa Rosa.*

## MITOTE FOOD PARK

**WHAT:** An authentic cultural and culinary experience in Santa Rosa's Latino district

**WHERE:** 665-777 Sebastopol Rd., Santa Rosa

**COST:** Free to see

**PRO TIP:** Look for the *Good vs. Evil* mural, a dramatic depiction of a Latina confronting a threatening, masked *lucha libre* wrestler.

Hungry families and tourists line up at Antojitos La Victoria to get massive quesadillas, and Gio y Los Magos Mexican Grill provides a menu based primarily on savory birria tacos, quesadillas, and tortas. Chicken on the grill, fresh crepes, hot churros, Cuban sandwiches, and kettle corn make El Mercadito Farmers Market smell like heaven while shoppers load up on fruits and veggies from local growers.

# A PLEA FOR PEACE

## Where is Benny's Peace Obelisk?

A startling sight as you drive along coast-hugging Highway 1, the vibrantly hued, 93-foot-tall tower depicting the Madonna and child and topped by a giant welcoming hand stands high on a stony hilltop at the Timber Cove Resort. Named the "Peace Obelisk" and completed in 1969, the sculpture was created over a seven-year period by Benjamino Bufano, a flamboyant and controversial artist known for expressing his antiwar sentiments with dramatic works of art and equally dramatic gestures, such as when he cut off his finger and sent it to President Woodrow Wilson in protest against the US entry into World War I.

Minimalist in style and constructed of concrete, mosaic tile, redwood, and lead, if the sculpture looks missile-like

### THE PEACE OBELISK

**WHAT:** An artful monument to peace overlooking the Pacific

**WHERE:** Above the Timber Cove Resort, 21780 N Coast Hwy. 1, Jenner

**COST:** Free

**PRO TIP:** You don't have to be a guest at the Timber Cove Resort to see Bufano's sculpture up close. Park in the lot north of the resort, and follow the path to the obelisk.

Just 60 feet in diameter, the Bufano Peace Statue Monument is the second smallest park in California.

*An artist famous for his pacifist views in the 1960s, Benjamin0 Bufano designed the Peace Obelisk, a 93-foot-tall tower depicting the Madonna and child, and topped by a giant welcoming hand. Left photo courtesy of Sonoma County Tourism, right photo courtesy of Timber Cove Resort*

to you, it's meant to. It was designed at the time of the Cuban missile crisis and the assassinations of the Kennedys, Malcolm X, and Martin Luther King Jr. Among his other pacifist-related works, Bufano also created *St. Francis of the Guns*, at City College of San Francisco, which represents a saint wearing a robe of mosaic tiles upon which are the faces of Abraham Lincoln, King, and the Kennedys. The 20-ton obelisk was his last and largest work. He suffered a heart attack during the construction and died soon after the sculpture was erected.

# RUSSIAN TOTEMS

## What are those carved wooden posts in the park?

To honor their ancestors' connection to the 19th-century settlement of Fort Ross, artisans from Yakutsk, in the Sakha Republic in far northeastern Russia, came to the Gualala Point Regional Park in 2012 to create ceremonial totem posts, known as *serge* (pronounced "sayrgay"). They carved 40-foot-tall Douglas fir trunks in intricate traditional designs and erected them in a meadow during the summer solstice, along with blessings, dancing, and shamanic rituals.

Serges are horse hitching posts and spiritual symbols placed near homes, and the designs symbolize the desire for survival through climatic and natural disasters, just as much a challenge today as it was 200+ years ago when Yakutians helped to build Fort Ross, near here, for the Russians. The posts also represent a "tree of life" and a hope for ongoing generations. The Yakutian delegation returned in two years to participate in a weeklong Days of Sakha Culture festival of art and performances.

## YAKUTIAN TOTAMS

**WHAT:** The only Yakutian serge posts outside of Russia

**WHERE:** 42401 Coast Hwy. 1, Gualala

**COST:** $7 parking fee

**PRO TIP:** Serge posts were also created and installed elsewhere on the coast at Timber Cove Inn and the Gualala Art Center.

The name Gualala comes from the Kashaya Pomo phrase, *ah kha wa la lee* which means "where the water flows down."

Left: *Ceremonial totem posts, known as serges, were hand-carved and erected at Gualala Point Regional Park and at Fort Ross.*

Right: *Part of a delegation from Republic Sakha (Yakutia) in Russia, a Yakutian shaman participated in rituals and dances at the Gualala Arts Center to commemorate the installation of the totems at Gualala Point Regional Park. Photo courtesy of the Gualala Art Center*

Just south of the border with Mendocino County and the town of Gualala, the Gualala River flows into the regional park on its way to the Pacific, then north into an estuary alongside a long sandbar. On the river side, you can wade and swim in warm water (in summer), explore cattail marshes, observe osprey nests, and go fishing or kayaking. On the ocean side, you can build a driftwood fort, roll down sand dunes, and bird-watch. The park also has walking trails and a campground in a redwood forest, plus a visitors center with displays of early Native American history, the Gualala River, and the marine environment.

# THE AMERICAN DREAM

### Where is the first winery in the United States founded by migrant farm workers?

Although Mexican vineyard workers have long been the foundation of the California wine industry, few wineries are owned by Mexican Americans. The very first winery established by former migrant workers from Mexico, the Robledo Family Winery in the Sonoma Valley, is a unique destination for wine lovers. When exploring the grounds of the gracious Mission-style tasting room and winery, if you see people wearing cowboy boots and Stetson hats, they are likely family members, as several generations are involved in the winery operation.

At age 16, Reynaldo Robledo emigrated from Michoacán to the United States in 1968, joining his father who was on the Bracero Program, a US work-visa plan enabling workers to legally cross the border. Reynaldo learned to farm and graft grapevines, became a foreman, and eventually traveled to Spain, France, and Morocco to teach the grafting techniques that he invented. Heralding his grafting innovations and his family history, his black cowboy hat (which he wore when he met President Obama), his grafting toolbox, and other artifacts are on exhibit in the National Museum of American History in Washington, DC.

Reynaldo and his wife, Maria, purchased property in the Los Carneros appellation and planted Pinot Noir grapes. Today, the

---

If you just can't bear to leave the wine country, you can book the three-bedroom, ranch-style Robledo Farm Stay house at the winery through Airbnb.

*The Robledo Family Winery is the first winery in the US founded by migrant farm workers from Mexico. Three generations of the family welcome visitors for wine tasting and tours at their hacienda-style estate in Sonoma. Photos courtesy of Robledo Family Winery*

## ROBLEDO FAMILY WINERY

**WHAT:** Mexican American history and award-winning Sonoma County wines

**WHERE:** 21901 Bonness Rd., Sonoma

**COST:** Free to see

**PRO TIP:** Among annual events are the lobster and shrimp boil in September, when Maine lobsters are heaped onto paper-clad tables for guests to crack open and enjoy with award-winning Robledo wines.

family owns more than 450 acres of vineyards in three counties. (Ironically, the name Los Carneros, "the rams" in Spanish, dates from the 1830s, when Mexico controlled Alta California.) The matriarch of the winery, Maria, owns and farms her own vineyards, and she was featured in the 2019 documentary, *Harvest Season*, nationally broadcasted on PBS.

# FOUNDER OF SONOMA

## Is there a home in Sonoma fit for a general?

In 1851, a fanciful Carpenter Gothic–style Victorian house was shipped, in pieces, around the Horn from New England to Alta California to become the home of General Mariano Guadalupe Vallejo, the Mexican Director of Colonization of the Northern Frontier. He and his wife and 16 children lived at Lachryma Montis ("mountain tears") for more than 35 years, while he commanded a contingent of Mexican troops; founded a pueblo named Sonoma (meaning "Valley of the Moon"); laid out a plaza and a grid of streets, which remain today; and used the formerly Catholic mission church as his headquarters.

Today part of the Sonoma State Historic Park, the charming yellow-and-white house and outbuildings are museums filled with vintage photos, authentic furnishings, everyday artifacts, and a sweet carriage ordered from France. Each room has

### GENERAL VALLEJO'S HOME

**WHAT:** Home of General Mariano Guadalupe Vallejo

**WHERE:** 363 3rd St. W, Sonoma

**COST:** $3 adults, $2 ages 6–16, free for under 5; tickets are good on the same day for the multisite Sonoma State Historic Park and the Petaluma Adobe.

**PRO TIP:** Steps from the Vallejo home is a 1.5-mile-long walking path running along the north side of Sonoma.

Once housing Vallejo's soldiers, steps from the mission are their restored adobe barracks, where you'll find historic exhibits on display and the State Park's gift shop.

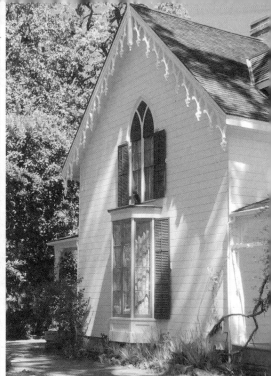

*Named Lachryma Montis ("mountain tears"), a "pre-fab" Carpenter Gothic-style house was shipped around the Horn from New England to what is today Sonoma to become the home of General Mariano Guadalupe Vallejo.*

a white marble fireplace and lace curtains, while parlors have crystal chandeliers, a rosewood grand piano, period clothing, toys, elaborately decorated saddles, and more. The library at one point contained 12,000 books; and, Vallejo himself added to that number by writing a five-volume history of California late in life, before his death in 1890.

The tree-shaded fish pond is still fed by a spring for which the home was named, and above the pond is the hideaway of Vallejo's youngest son, Napoleon, who lived with a gang of pets—more than a dozen dogs, several cats, a parrot—and his hunting rifle.

After the Treaty of Guadalupe Hidalgo was signed in 1848, making Alta California part of the United States, Vallejo went on to become a state senator and a pioneering grape grower and winemaker.

# RHODIES IN BLOOM

## Where can we see wild rhododendrons?

The cool, misty Pacific Coast climate is perfect not only for redwood and fir forests but also for a particular grove of dazzling pink- and magenta-blooming rhododendrons. Originally part of a ranch in the 1880s, on which the Kruse family raised sheep and harvested logs, a unique 317-acre redwood and fir woodland habitat for forest and flora was donated to the state of California in the 1930s, to become the Kruse Rhododendron State Natural Reserve. Mid-April through mid-June, the park is wildly ablaze with native *rhododendron macrophyllum* that burst into bouquets of bell-shaped, brilliant pink-to-dark-rose-purple blooms, dramatic against the dark green backdrop. About five miles of easy trails weave through the reserve, when in winter and springtime, streams and waterfalls burble through the fern glens and oceans

### KRUSE RHODODENDRON STATE NATURAL RESERVE

**WHAT:** A native garden of brilliant pink-blooming rhododendrons and wildflowers

**WHERE:** 25050 Hwy. 1, 21 miles north of Jenner

**COST:** Free

**PRO TIP:** Are you a rhodie lover? Visit Hidden Forest Nursery in Sebastopol, where acres of rhodies, azaleas, and camellias thrive in a tree-shaded canyon threaded with footpaths.

Just south of Gualala, the rhodie preserve is within Salt Point State Park and near several accessible beaches.

*Hundreds of acres of redwood and fir woodland is sheltering habitat for wild rhododendrons that burst into brilliant pink bloom in late spring. Photos courtesy of Sonoma County Tourism*

of wildflowers. The vibrant rhodies compete with wild orchids and iris, fairy slippers, violets, and elegant white trillium.

For a short overview, take the 2.25-mile loop trail that passes on little bridges over Chinese Gulch and Phillips Gulch, both adorned with small waterfalls; watch for signs to a longer hike.

Nearby, take shelter from the wind at the Fisk Mill Cove picnic site, and walk to Sentinel Rock for colossal coastal views.

# THE WORLD OF *PEANUTS*

## Who is Sparky Schulz?

Celebrating the life of the *Peanuts* characters and their creator, Charles (Sparky) Schulz, the Charles M. Schulz Museum is one of the most popular tourist attractions in the county, where the cartoonist lived and worked for more than four decades. Within 8,000 square feet of impressive contemporary architecture is the largest collection of *Peanuts* artwork in the world. Here you'll find 100+ original comic strips on view at any one time, along with extensive memorabilia, a re-creation of Schulz's studio, and dramatic art installations, from a massive bas relief sculpture to a 22-foot-long mural composed of 3,588 *Peanuts* images on little ceramic tiles.

Kids head right for the theater to watch animated TV specials and other films, and to the education building where they learn to draw and animate cartoons, color *Peanuts* characters, make an origami doghouse, and participate in special learning days. Selfies are sensational in the courtyard by the "kite-eating tree" and life-size replicas of all the characters. Look down into the birdbath to see holographic images of Snoopy and Woodstock.

Adjacent to the museum are "Snoopy's Home Ice" Redwood Ice Arena, designed by Schulz, who was also an ice hockey player; and Snoopy's Gallery and Gift Shop, a mecca for *Peanuts* fans, with a stained-glass rose window and murals featuring

### CHARLES M. SCHULZ MUSEUM

**WHAT:** The home, art, and history of the *Peanuts* cartoon characters and their creator and hometown hero

**WHERE:** 2301 Hardies Ln., Santa Rosa

**COST:** Free ages 3 and under; $5 ages 4–18; $8 ages 62 and over; $12 adults

**PRO TIP:** Next door, the Children's Museum of Sonoma County keeps kids busy with hands-on art, nature, and science projects.

*Peanuts cartoon characters and their creator are celebrated in a vast museum of artful exhibits related to Charlie Brown, Lucy, and the gang. Avid Peanuts fans head for Snoopy's Gallery and Gift Shop. Photos courtesy of Charles M. Schulz Museum*

Snoopy and Woodstock. On hand are dolls, logo clothing (such as Charlie Brown's zigzag shirt), toys, books, and much more.

"My name is Charlie Brown. All my friends refer to me as 'Good Ol' Charlie Brown.'"

At the Warm Puppy Café, one table remains reserved for Sparky, who dined here most days, watching the ice skaters through the large windows. Peppermint Patty hot chocolate, Charlie Brownies, and Good Grief Grilled Cheese are popular menu items.

# WE'RE STILL HERE!

## Where are the Coffey Park murals?

In 2017, a wildfire destroyed thousands of homes in Sonoma and Napa Counties, including in Santa Rosa, where the entire 1,200-home neighborhood of Coffey Park was wiped out in one night. Today, Coffey Park is back and better than ever in a miraculous emergence from the ashes, devastation, and grief; the new neighborhood is a showcase of new homes, luxuriant yards, and tree-lined streets. As a grand expression of the resilience of these neighbors coming together to rebuild their community, a new 5.9-acre park was built, complete with water features, outdoor sculptures, state-of-the-art playgrounds and vast lawns, fitness equipment, and picnic grounds. Coffey Park is back, big time.

In celebration of the resilience and spirit of the reborn neighborhood and the town, along a street that borders Coffey Park, seven long, flamboyantly colorful, hand-painted murals

### SANTA ROSA RESILIENCE

**WHAT:** A street full of vibrant murals heralding the rebirth of a neighborhood ravaged by fire

**WHERE:** 1021 Hopper Ave., Santa Rosa

**COST:** Free

**PRO TIP:** Drive west past the murals to the Coffey Neighborhood Park on Coffey Lane to enjoy the playground (there's a dog park too).

---

If your family loves playgrounds, don't miss Howarth Park in Santa Rosa, where an elaborate set of play structures is augmented by a little steam train, a carousel, and a petting zoo.

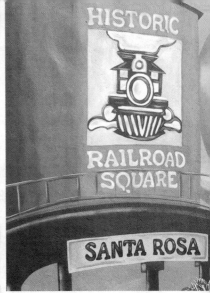

Seven flamboyantly colorful, hand-painted murals depict Santa Rosa's history, celebrating the resilience and spirit of the town and the neighborhood of Coffey Park after the disastrous fires of 2017.

now grace the previously unremarkable stretch of walls enclosing a storage company. The murals depict Santa Rosa's history, from steam locomotives to a redwood forest and hot-air balloons. Featured is hometown hero Charles Schulz, creator of the *Peanuts* cartoons; horticulturist Luther Burbank; the county's legendary Pacific coastline; the microbrewery industry; a Historic District; and the Pacific Coast Air Museum.

Inspired as a child by the *Peanuts* characters, the muralist, Jerry Ragg, has created thousands of murals across the United States, including this one for the Santa Rosa company, Security Public Storage.

# GIANT REDWOODS

## What is the tallest tree on earth?

As the tallest and some of the oldest trees on earth, coast redwoods exist only in a narrow band along the Northern California and Oregon coastlines and a few miles inland, with magnificent groves in the "Redwood Empire" of Northern California. At the Armstrong Grove State Natural Reserve in Guerneville, first-timers can see and learn about the giants on the self-guided Pioneer Nature Trail, a flat 1.5-mile loop, which is ADA accessible and dotted with interpretive signs.

The trees can live 2,000 years or more, and reach up to 379 feet tall and nearly 30 feet in diameter. The Parson Jones Tree here is 310 feet tall—longer than a football field, while the oldest, the 1,400-year-old Colonel Armstrong Tree, is named for the

### ARMSTRONG GROVE STATE NATURAL RESERVE

**WHAT:** Reserve threaded with 9+ miles of footpaths in 805 acres of endangered coast redwoods

**WHERE:** 17000 Armstrong Woods Rd., Guerneville

**COST:** $10 per vehicle (or park at the entrance and walk in for free)

**PRO TIP:** Wheelchair access, a Braille trail, and biking and equestrian trails are available. Dogs on leashes are allowed only on the paved road and in one of the developed picnic areas.

This reserve is a living monument to the two million acres of primeval redwood forests that blanketed Northern California before the logging of the 19th century; less than 5% of the original forests remain.

*Thousands of towering redwoods in the Armstrong Grove are some of the last precious stands of the trees in Northern California's "Redwood Empire."*

lumberman who set the groves aside for the public in the 1870s. The Icicle Tree shows the mysterious burl formations that can weigh tons.

A springtime walk among the towering trunks can be enchanting, when the forest floor is carpeted with creamy-white trilliums, fairy bells, and purple-pink orchids. Summertime is also magical, when Fife Creek is bubbling, and picnic sites are cool beneath the high, dense canopy. In the fall, maples, alders, and buckeyes sparkle red and gold against the dark, cinnamon-colored bark, and come winter, mushrooms, mosses, and lichens show off their vibrant multicolors. Look for the tree-hugging platforms!

# A GREEN DREAM OF A WINERY

## What is biodynamic farming?

More than two decades ago, on the slopes of Sonoma Mountain near Glen Ellen, Benziger Family Winery became a pioneering, certified biodynamic farm, and it continues to be a showplace of sustainable grape growing and wine making. Their tractor-pulled, open-air tram tour, which shows off green farming practices from crop rotation to composting, and native flora, is repeatedly voted "Best Winery Tour." Sheep are out there mowing the cover crops, long-haired Scottish Highlander cattle are providing fertilizer, the vegetable garden is buzzing with bees, and bugs are busily vanquishing harmful organisms at the insectary. Keep your eyes peeled for the bird boxes, popular with owls and bats. Home-grown herbs are used to make enriching teas that are sprayed on the vines and soil, and irrigation water is recycled in the ponds you see, which are fed by natural springs. The tour goes on to the naturally cool cellar caves, the production facilities, and, finally, the tasting rooms.

With a reservation, you can also just taste some wine and wander around the estate on your own in the lush gardens.

---

### BENZIGER FAMILY WINERY

**WHAT:** One of the preeminent biodynamic wineries in the world

**WHERE:** 1883 London Ranch Rd., Glen Ellen

**COST:** From $30 per person depending on tasting experience and tours

**PRO TIP:** Take the free, self-guided, 100-yard Biodynamic Discovery Trail to learn about biodynamic farming. The path is lush with native plants, fruits and veggies, grapes, lavender, and a bubbling fountain in a pool.

*Tractor-pulled, open-air tram tours show off biodynamic farming practices at Benziger Family Winery, where sheep and cattle mow down the cover crops, and bees and bugs hobnob in the insectary. The educational tour also includes the cool cellar caves, the wine-making facilities, and the tasting salons. Photo courtesy of Benziger Family Winery*

Note the hundreds of olive trees that combat erosion on the hilly estate and produce fruit that is pressed into the oils, soaps, and lotions sold in the gift shop, where candle holders and other tabletop accessories were created from recycled wine barrels.

Claiming a Michelin Bib Gourmand rating with a wood oven–roasted menu, the Glen Ellen Star is co-owned by the daughter of Mike Benziger, the pioneering winemaker.

# OENOPHILES' HIDEAWAY

## Where did my wine lover disappear?

Quiet and filled with natural light and comfortable seating, the Sonoma County Wine Library is a little-known treasure chest for the wine-inclined. One of the nation's largest collections of wine-related books, oral histories, magazines, journals, photos, maps, labels, posters, and videos, this wine-lovers lair is tucked into the back of the Healdsburg Regional Library. Among the 6,000+ books are nearly a thousand rare volumes dating from 1850 to 1950. Printed by hand in Latin in 1514, the oldest and most valuable volume, *Libri de re Rustica*, is a detailed description of agricultural practices of the time.

Wine enthusiasts head for the maps of American Viticultural Areas (designated wine grape–growing regions), documentary films, and even wine-related murder mysteries. Among other books you'll find are *What Makes a Wine Worth Drinking* and *Flawless: Understanding Faults in Wine*, plus the popular movie, *Sideways*. The library also includes a collection of audio and video histories of Northern California winery owners and winemakers, as well as a fascinating collection of memorabilia of wineries around the county, from old letters and manuscripts to vintage photos, posters, and labels.

---

Friends of the Sonoma County Wine Library hosts events from wine tastings to talks by authors and winery luminaries.

Sonoma County Wine Library is one of the country's most comprehensive collections of wine-related books, oral histories, magazines, photos, maps, posters, and videos. Photos courtesy of Sonoma County Wine Library

## SONOMA COUNTY WINE LIBRARY

**WHAT:** The ultimate source of wine-tasting itineraries, winery histories, and vintage photos, books, and memorabilia related to wine and the wine industry

**WHERE:** 139 Piper St., Healdsburg

**COST:** Free

**PRO TIP:** The library has maps to wine-tasting rooms within easy walking distance of the library and the downtown plaza.

Locals and visitors plan their vacations here, delving into guidebooks to wine regions around the world, and discovering food-and-wine news in four dozen or so current periodicals, from journals of enology and viticulture to *Sonoma-Marin Farm News* and *Wine Spectator*.

# SONOMA CABLE CARS

### Who needs a designated driver?

Throwing worries about driving-while-wine-tasting to the wind, you can trundle around in safety and style to historic sites and premium wineries in a hand-built replica of a San Francisco cable car, just like those used in the city from the late 1890s to the early 1930s. Every detail, from the all-wooden carriage to the brass bell and the bright-red-and-gold decoration is right off the original blueprints. Departing from the Sonoma Plaza, groups or individuals climb aboard the open-air, motorized trolley car for six-hour, narrated tours that include private, leisurely tasting experiences at four award-winning Sonoma wineries, a catered lunch, and hobnobbing fun with like-minded wine-inclined people.

On a state-of-the-art sound system, the tour guide on the Sonoma Valley Wine Trolley explains the sites around Sonoma Plaza. Stopping for photo ops, you'll see Mission San Francisco Solano, the Bear Flag Monument, much of the Sonoma Historic State Park, and a unique city hall.

The trolley moves through the verdant valley to Glen Ellen grove, and wine tasting ensues at such Sonoma Valley notables as VJB Cellars, where after sipping hearty Italian varietals such as Barbera, Montepulciano and Aglianico, you can shop for the

## SONOMA VALLEY WINE TROLLEY

**WHAT:** Winery and history tours of Healdsburg on open-air motorized tolley cars

**WHERE:** 21707 8th St. E, Ste. B, Sonoma

**COST:** $99 per person, plus fees for the wine tastings

**PRO TIP:** For photo ops, the Sonoma Valley is best in the spring when yellow mustard blankets the vineyards and California poppies blaze orange across the hillsides. After the harvest and vacationers have gone home, late September and all of October are prime months for vineyard color, sparkling days, and warm nights.

*A hand-built replica of those in San Francisco, the Sonoma Cable Car cruises to historic sites and wineries in the Sonoma Valley. Photo courtesy of Sonoma Cable Cars*

artisan cheeses, house-made sauces, pestos, and estate-grown olive oils on offer at the Italian marketplace. Don't miss the Tommy Bahama boutique and the truffle and gelato shop.

Among the Wine Trolley's adventures on your tour may be Mayo Family Winery, known for small batch Old Vine Zinfandels; and Imagery Estate Winery where a gallery displays 60 or so of over 500 original art works that have been translated into dramatic labels on such unique wines as Noir Nouveau, Wow Red, and Code Blue. Here you can also play bocce and horseshoes.

The trolley tour may also include the sculpture gardens, the vast views, and Russian River Valley wines at Paradise Ridge Winery, or the wine history museum at Buena Vista, California's oldest premium winery.

The tour stops for selfie-taking spots such as the bench next to General Vallejo in the plaza.

# THE OLD TRADERS' TRAIL

## Where on the coast did the early Pomo people live?

Thousands of years ago, some of the earliest known human settlements were along the Sonoma coastline, on riverbanks and near beaches. Villages of the Coast Pomo tribe were near the mouth of the Russian River and also at the eastern end of today's Pomo Canyon Trail, which you can hike, as you imagine the abundant, pristine environment that provided their sustenance.

The Pomo were traders, along with Miwok and Wappo tribes, who trod this same trail with their baskets and their takings from the ocean, which they gathered in the warmer months by fishing and collecting crabs, mussels, abalone, and seaweed. The ancient footpath between Shell Beach and the Pomo Canyon Campground remains today and zigzags about seven miles or so round trip through oak, laurel, and fir woodlands, crossing seeps and streams. You'll want to stop at the magical redwood grove by a stream, adorned with

Since the 1800s and still today, Pomo tribal members have been world famous for their basketry, which is exhibited at the Jesse Peter Multicultural Museum in Santa Rosa.

*A redwood grove by a stream, wildflowery meadows, and dazzling coastal views adorn the footpath from Shell Beach into the foothills. Photo courtesy of Golden Gate National Park Conservancy*

*A moderate 6.2-mile hiking trail from Shell Beach to the Pomo Canyon Campground. Photo courtesy of Visit Jenner*

*On the Pomo Canyon Trail, a shady redwood grove by a stream adorned with ferns and wildflowers. Photo courtesy of Sonoma State University*

### Pomo Canyon Trail
#### Campground to Shell Beach
Sonoma Coast State Park

ferns and wildflowers. From a bench at the top of the trail, you can see down the coast in both directions.

Back at your starting point at small, pretty, "tide-pooly" Shell Beach, on weekends, you may well encounter docents from the State Park Roving Naturalist Program, who will tell you all about marine ecology and Pomo history.

**131**

# BRAIN FREEZE IS WORTH IT

## What do frozen soursop and chongo taste like?

One of the delights of this county's Latino population is their unique Michoacana-style ice cream, which comes from a long tradition. Known as the Mexican capital of *helado* (ice cream) and fresh fruit *paletas* (ice pops), the small town of Tocumbo in the state of Michoacan originated in the mid-1940s the home-made, 100%-natural Michoacana-style ice cream that you now find here and all over Mexico. These ice creams are all made from scratch from fresh fruits and spices, with less fat and air than American ice creams, and although rich and creamy, they are not made with heavy cream.

More than 15,000 La Michoacana *paleterías* (popsicle shops) and helado stores are located in Mexico, and most of them are owned by people from Tocumbo. So many town residents work in or own paleterías that a two-story monument of a paleta and a scoop of helado stands at the entrance to the town.

You can't miss La Michoacana here in Sonoma, where a vivid pink-and-orange facade announces this little shop on Highway 12. Exotic flavors such as soursop (zesty pineapple and papaya taste), rose petal, *rompope* (eggnog), Nutella, and pine nut are created in-house, and Mexican vanilla is a favorite.

---

When at local festivals and farm markets, keep your eyes peeled for a yellow-and-white trailer emblazoned "Trader Jim's Whips, Floats, Soft Serve." The pineapple whips are nondairy soft-serves, with or without a float of fresh pineapple juice.

## MEXICAN-STYLE ICE CREAM

**WHAT:** Exotic flavors in Mexican-style homemade ice cream

**WHERE:** Around the county

**COST:** Depends on how many scoops!

**PRO TIP:** Along Highway 12 in the Latino district of Sonoma, several buildings sport wildly vivid paint jobs across their storefronts, from the much-larger-than-life-sized rooster on El Brinquito Market to Tienda Y Panaderia Iniguez's cornucopia of fruits.

Top: *In Sonoma, La Michoacana specializes in Mexican-style ice cream.*

Bottom: *In a Victorian-era former bank on Main Street, Nimble & Finn's in Guerneville is famous for exotic flavors such as Maple Bourbon Bacon Brittle, Honeyed Peach, Rhubarb Crisp, Lavender, Meyer Lemon, and more homemade ice creams.*

Besides fruit paletas, Frozen Art in Santa Rosa specializes in Mexican flavors such as *horchata*, avocado, *chongos*, cheese, passion fruit, mango, and dozens more. In addition, in four locations, Fru-Ta's menu leans toward tropical fruits, from guava and papaya to guanaba, *chongo zamorano* (caramel custardy), tequila (not exactly a fruit), and *pastelito* (cake).

# WEST COUNTY CHARM

## How do you find a village lost in time?

Tucked away on a narrow country road, the tiny village of Graton is home to overgrown gardens, timeworn cottages, and a line-up of 19th-century false-front buildings reminiscent of a Western movie set. A lively farming town in the 1800s heydays of Gravenstein apple production, today's block-long hamlet is a sweet 21st-century discovery with an impressive art gallery, wine-tasting venues, nationally acclaimed eateries, and antiques shops.

Like an aging, yet dignified, dowager at the top of the town, the Graton Community Club is the glue that holds the community of about 1,800 together. A former chicken hatchery, in 1916, the building was hauled by horses to where it presides today, hosting teas, weddings, town hall meetings, election debates, and the biggest annual event in town, the Spring Flower Show. For the show, locals grow vegetable seedlings and potted plants; spend months creating handmade quilts, crafts, toys, and birdhouses; and collect white elephant treasures. The proceeds go to scholarships for West County kids.

---

Graton Road meanders west over rolling hills to Miramar Estate, owned by a member of a Spanish wine dynasty. Just 10 miles from the Pacific Ocean, sunset on the patio is the place to be, with a glass of Green Valley Pinot Noir in hand.

*Reminiscent of its heydays of the 1800s, the former apple-raising village of Graton is today an art colony and a cache of eateries, boutique shops, and wine-tasting salons, anchored by the Graton Community Club.*

## VILLAGE OF GRATON

**WHAT:** Old-fashioned charms in the village of Graton

**WHERE:** Graton Road off Hwy. 116 between Forestville and Sebastopol

**COST:** Free

**PRO TIP:** On the east end of town, Bowman Cellars' shiny Airstream RV serves snacks to wine tasters as they relax in the gardens.

The other big event is the Graton Day Parade, a quirky convoy of decorated convertibles and flatbed trucks, along with hometown bands, culminating in a street party, pet parade, and pie contest.

On the west end at the Hallberg building stands "Captain CAB" and his pirate booty, guarding Purple Wine + Spirits in a circa-1947 apple-processing plant turned wine warehouse. Hallberg arrived from Sweden in 1886 and planted 1,000+ acres of apple orchards. Although most orchards are now vineyards, heritage apples and hard cider are reviving the attention of local farmers and foodies.

# GEOLOGICAL WONDER

## What was that explosion in the Pliocene?

Imagine a dense, thriving redwood forest three million years ago, and then imagine it turned to stone by the violent eruptions of Mount Saint Helena. Those redwoods are petrified today, as they have been since the Pliocene, and you can see them in their silvery-gray magnificence at the Petrified Forest, a California Historical Landmark on the eastern edge of the county. These are the largest petrified trees in the world; the "Queen," already 2,000 years old when the volcano blew it's top, is 8 feet wide and 65 feet long. You'll see the "Monarch," once more than 100 feet tall, and also a tree named for Robert Louis Stevenson, who in the late 1880s described it in his book, *The Silverado Squatters*.

Ongoing eruptions buried the trees in ash, cutting off oxygen for millennia, while water seeped into the cellular spaces of the trees, creating silica, which turned the trees into perfectly preserved fossils. Over the years, research on the property

### PETRIFIED FOREST

**WHAT:** 3 million-year-old redwood forest

**WHERE:** 4100 Petrified Forest Rd., Santa Rosa

**COST:** Adults $12, students $8, kids $6, under 6 free

**PRO TIP:** The Petrified Forest gift shop exhibits and sells semiprecious stones, fossils, and minerals from around the world.

Just up the road at Hans Fahden Vineyards, a tea house in a Monet-style garden with a lily pond is a cool and pleasant place to taste wine, vinted here since 1912.

*Victims of a volcanic eruption 3 million years ago, dozens of massive redwood trees are preserved as they fell. Today's Petrified Forest is a California Historical Landmark. Photos courtesy of Petrified Forest*

through the University of California has also turned up petrified pine and oak trees, and fossil leaf impressions of other conifers and hardwoods. Frozen in time right where they fell those eons ago, the massive fossils retain the imprint of their original bark, growth rings, and burls.

You can take a guided tour, or just take a walk on the flat, 1.5-mile loop Meadow Trail, which promises meadows, of course, and a view of Mount Saint Helena, the now extinct perpetrator of death and destruction.

# CHAPEL BY THE SEA

## Is that building about to fly away?

Seeming about to sail out from within a dense pine, redwood, and oak forest, the Sea Ranch Chapel is a winged wonder that appears suspended high above the Pacific near Gualala. Designed by James Hubbell in 1985 and created by local craftspeople and artisans, the tiny nondenominational chapel was built as a complement to the rambling Sea Ranch residential development that is laid out for several miles along the coastline.

Perched on a dramatic stone base, locally felled cedar creates the overlapping exterior siding and the swooping roof shingles, which are topped by a verdigris patina copper sculpture of a bird's wing.

Within the 360-square-foot interior, designed to

## SEA RANCH CHAPEL

**WHAT:** A hand-built, craftsman-created seaside chapel of architectural interest

**WHERE:** 40033 CA-1, Sea Ranch, 50 miles north of Jenner on Hwy. 1 at mile marker 55.66, across from Bosun's Reach St.

**COST:** Free

**PRO TIP:** The light-filled, unique, and intimate venue is often used for small weddings.

One of the most restrictive residential developments ever built in California, the several hundred homes of Sea Ranch are hidden in evergreen groves and tall, native grasses, widely scattered and naturally weathered, some with sod roofs.

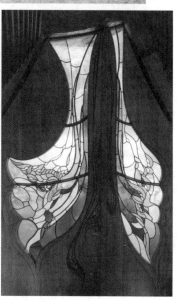

*High above the Pacific, created by local craftspeople, a tiny, architecturally striking chapel rich with glowing stained glass, mosaics, and copper and iron adornments. Bottom left photo courtesy of the Sea Ranch Chapel, bottom right photo courtesy of Sonoma County Tourism*

seat just 40 people, are eye-popping enhancements such as glowing stained-glass windows, a literally sparkling mosaic and stone floor, and a whimsical ceiling decorated with seashells. An elaborate wrought iron prayer screen and chandelier are among countless artistic touches. Local stone is used on the exterior, interior, and courtyard.

Outside the chapel, be sure to sit on the redwood bench to catch the sunset over the sea.

# BLINK AND YOU'LL MISS IT

## Is it a town, a village, or a stop in the road?

Springing out of a northern mountain range, the Russian River rambles more than 100 miles before it slides into the Pacific at Jenner, where a clutch of cottages and sea views call for a visit. The mouth of the river creates a tranquil, shallow estero with sandy shoals where migrating birds gather in the thousands and harbor seals lounge to give birth away from the sharp eyes of hungry sharks and whales. Hundreds of pups are born between January and June, and as cute as they are, visitors and their dogs are required to stay at least 50 feet away.

Overlooking the wildlife action, the deck and the Adirondack chairs of Café Aquatica are catbird seats from which to watch playful otters, swooping pelicans, cormorants, seagulls, barking seals, and kayakers plying the calm lagoon. Crashing waves and sea stacks, and sometimes whales, draw the eye along the coastline.

In an old boathouse, the Jenner Visitors Center is a nature store with history and wildlife displays, along with brochures of places to eat, stay, and explore along the coast, with State Park docents are on hand to advise. Seashells, wind chimes, and sweatshirts for blustery days are available at Jenner Sea Gifts & Wine, where you can sit by the firepit on the outdoor deck, sipping wine as the sun sinks over the horizon.

## JENNER BY THE SEA

**WHAT:** Where the Russian River meets the sea, a mini village, with harbor seals providing the entertainment

**WHERE:** 10439 Hwy. 1, Jenner

**COST:** Free to see

**PRO TIP:** Launch your kayak or canoe to explore the calm estuary, or rent kayaks from Watertreks, where you can also book paddling tours and full-moon paddles.

Top left: *Jenner Headlands Preserve is a 5,630-acre woodland and prairie with hiking trails and a mounted telescope for whale-watching. Photo courtesy of The Wildlands Conservancy*

Top right: *A village of clapboard cottages, Jenner by the Sea looks onto the Pacific. Photo courtesy of Visit Sonoma Coast*

Bottom left: *Café Aquatica in Jenner has a deck and garden patio where patrons are mesmerized by views of the lagoon and the open sea.*

Bottom right: *The mouth of the Russian River meets the Pacific Ocean at Jenner by the Sea. Photo courtesy of Visit Sonoma Coast*

Just up the road, Jenner Headlands Preserve is a 5,630-acre woodland and prairie with a mounted telescope for whale-watching and a short, accessible paved trail. Hikers can hit the 15-mile round-trip trail up Pole Mountain.

# WILDLIFE AND WASTEWATER

## Is that a sewage treatment plant over there?

Think of sewage, then think of vast marshy wetlands where "black" water flows into ponds and mudflats and is miraculously "polished" by plants that remove metals, chemicals, and other toxins. The result is clean habitat for wildlife; recycled water for local parks, golf courses, and farms; and a magical public park. With Petaluma's Ellis Creek wastewater recycling facility in the distance, miles of flat trails in Shollenberger Park wind through a watery wonderland alive with waterfowl, and resident and migratory birds and raptors. A one-mile trail also leads from the park over Adobe Creek through Alman Marsh, ending at the Sheraton Sonoma Wine Country hotel.

On the several brackish ponds and in the mud flats, and amid the thick stands of bulrushes and cattails, you'll see some 200+ species of birds and ducks, from egrets and teal to killdeer, curlew, ibis, bitterns, phalaropes, and lots of geese. Nesting and breeding happens from April to July, especially among great egrets, snowy egrets, and great blue herons.

Birds of prey, including several types of hawks, peregrine falcons, ravens, and the occasional eagle and owl, swoop and

## SHOLLENBERGER PARK WETLANDS

**WHAT:** Wastewater treatment results in a walkable wetlands park.

**WHERE:** 3882 Cypress Dr., Petaluma

**COST:** Free

**PRO TIP:** The Petaluma Wetlands Alliance offers tours of the park and the *Petaluma Wetlands Field Guide.*

Top: *Petaluma's wastewater facility turns recycled water into a watery wonderland alive with waterfowl.*

Top inset: *Avocets stalk the ponds and wetlands of Schollenberger Park, created by recycled water from the adjacent wastewater plant.*

Bottom inset: *Tree swallows and owls are residents of bird boxes in the wetlands of Schollenberger Park in Petaluma. Photos courtesy of Petaluma Wetlands Alliance.*

nest in the tall eucalyptus trees. Interpretive signs picture the wildlife and explain the incredible process of turning "black" water into clean water, naturally, with no odor whatsoever!

Petaluma's wetlands provide habitat for endangered and threatened species such as the clapper rail, salt marsh harvest mouse, black rail, and western pond turtle.

# RUNNING WITH CHRISTO

## Why is that white ribbon running over the hills?

Just imagine more than 24 miles of billowing, translucent white fabric flowing from a major highway all the way to the Pacific Ocean where it plunged into the sea. Following the contours of the rolling hills of Sonoma County, in 1976, the 18-foot-tall *Running Fence* was one of the first spectacular, temporary art installations created by Christo, a conceptual artist. He went on for decades afterwards to drape dramatic floods of fabric onto monuments, in parks, across mountain passes, and over huge buildings.

Looking like a skinny hippie from the 1960s, with a wild mop of hair and horn-rimmed glasses, Christo Vladimirov Javacheff, a Bulgarian, cajoled, charmed, and convinced nearly 60 property owners and county officials that the fence must run, in spite of the Committee to Stop the Running Fence and other civic challenges. Finally, strung up on 2,050 poles with 90 miles of steel cable, comprising 240,000 square yards of white nylon and erected by a gang of volunteers, the fence meandered gracefully around roads, ranches, trees, and grazing cattle on its dramatic journey to the Pacific. After being seen by thousands of people walking, driving, and flying overhead, and being documented in detail in photographs and in Christo's sketches and paintings, the *Running Fence* was removed two weeks later by the same volunteers.

The Museum of Sonoma County is the home of an extensive collection of Christo's drawings, sculptures, and collages, along with photos and videos of many of his installations.

Temporary art installation Running Fence
by Christo in Sonoma County. Top photo
courtesy of Sonoma County Library

## CHRISTO'S
## *RUNNING FENCE*

**WHAT:** A look back at Christo's
*Running Fence*

**WHERE:** In museum collections
and documentary films

**COST:** Free

**PRO TIP:** In western Sonoma
County at the Valley Ford post
office stands one of the poles
from *Running Fence*, along with
a descriptive plaque.

Pioneering the genre of monumental outdoor art installations,
Christo also stretched a bright-orange curtain across a steep
mountain pass at Rifle Gap in the Rocky Mountains. Among his
most famous works were millions of square feet of floating pink
fabric surrounding islands on Biscayne Bay, 3,100 vivid golden
umbrellas in Japan, and 7,500 gates of saffron-colored panels in
New York City's Central Park.

# REDWOODS ON THE FAIRWAY

## Where did Bing play golf?

Northwood Golf Course just west of Guerneville was designed in 1928 by the Scottish architect Alister MacKenzie, already famous for laying out courses in the British Isles. He was lured to California to design Northwood for the pleasure of the nearby Bohemian Club encampment, which was, and still is, the site of annual summertime gatherings of politicians, world leaders, show-business greats, and corporate magnates; the golfers among them are often seen on MacKenzie's scenic nine-holer.

He went on to design Augusta National, Cypress Point, and countless more courses that remain renowned, even today. Here at Northwood, near the Russian River, hundreds of towering redwoods and firs stand along the fairways in misty magnificence, impervious to golf balls bouncing off their 150-foot-tall trunks, their long arms drooping over small greens well-guarded by mounds and bunkers.

A teenaged caddy at Northwood in the 1940s, Rich Quistgard recalled carrying Bing Crosby's golf bag. Not a bad player, Crosby asked for his "niblick" (today's nine iron), his

During World War I, MacKenzie studied military camouflage, which he related to golf course design. He wrote, "The whole secret of successful golf course construction and concealment in trench-making consists in making artificial features indistinguishable from natural ones."

*Designed in 1928 by the world famous Scottish architect Alister MacKenzie, Northwood Golf Course continues to challenge players whose golf balls have a tendency to hit the towering redwood trees. Bottom photo courtesy of Sonoma County Library*

# NORTHWOOD GOLF COURSE

**WHAT:** A rare, legendary golf course in a pristine redwood forest

**WHERE:** 19400 Hwy. 116, Monte Rio

**COST:** $32 for 9 holes, $45 for 18

**PRO TIP:** Even nongolfers stop for breakfast, lunch, and dinner on the sunny deck at the rustic bar and restaurant overlooking the first tee and the 10th green.

"mashie niblick" (a seven iron), and his "spoon" (a three-wood). In those days, the usual tip for a caddy was $1.25. When called away by a phone call after only three holes, the gracious Crosby handed the wide-eyed teen a $20 bill. Another big tipper was the American baritone, John Charles Thomas, who walked the Northwood fairways while singing arias from *La Traviata*.

# JAPANESE-STYLE SERENITY

## Feel like taking a bath in sawdust?

It's not like a mud bath or a soak in a Jacuzzi or a hot springs pool. The little-known, Japanese-style, deep-heating ritual of the cedar-enzyme bath originated in the 1940s on the island of Hokkaido, where health and wellness seekers slipped into wooden tubs filled with warm, soft, fluffy, aromatic concoctions and emerged energized and healed of their ailments. Beyond Japan, the unique baths are offered in just a handful of places in the world.

As the only spa on this continent that specializes in cedar-enzyme baths, Osmosis Day Spa Sanctuary in Freestone imports finely ground Port Orford cedar, vitamin-rich rice bran, and plant enzymes, and ferments this concoction with a Japanese catalyst into a hot, steaming, healing substance in tubs surrounded by a magical garden. The creator of the spa studied landscape gardening and Zen meditation in Kyoto, joined a Buddhist monastery, and discovered the traditional baths, which he found relieved his painful sciatica and other conditions. Returning to the United States, he discovered an isolated glen in western Sonoma County where, today, a creek runs alongside pagodas, pools, and elaborate, authentic Japanese-inspired gardens designed by Robert Ketchell, then president of Britain's Japanese Garden Society.

## OSMOSIS SANCTUARY

**WHAT:** A Japanese-style spa on the way to the coast

**WHERE:** 209 Bohemian Hwy., Freestone

**COST:** From $119 per person

**PRO TIP:** Just across the highway, Wild Flour Bakery is famous for wood-fired brick oven–baked breads, scones, and biscotti sold only here, Friday to Monday.

*Osmosis in Freestone is the only spa on this continent specializing in the deep heating rituals of the Japanese-style cedar-enzyme bath. Photos courtesy of Osmosis Sanctuary*

The stress-relieving qualities of the cedar treatment, the tea ceremony, and various optional treatments, including massage and "sound therapy," comprise a powerful combination for guests craving serenity, followed by a rest in a padded hammock on the creek side, and an exploration of the 10-stage meditation garden.

Cedar-enzyme baths gained international attention during the Winter Olympic Games in 1972 when used in the Sapporo athletes' village.

# OLD RAILROAD DAYS

## What is Richardsonian Romanesque?

The first narrow-gauge trains arrived in 1886 at the Kenwood Depot, the Sonoma Valley's primary railroad station until 1934, when rail service gave way to the automobile. Today, taking pride of place in the Wine Country village of Kenwood, the depot lies on a country road by a vineyard. A Historic Landmark, the fancifully designed stone building now serves the small community as a venue for events. Built of locally quarried, reddish-colored basalt stone, and one of only two stone depots of that era remaining in the state, the edifice claims "Richardsonian Romanesque" style, a unique takeoff on classic Romanesque created by Henry Hobson Richardson, known for designing Trinity Church in Boston.

Note the set-back entrance beneath an eyebrow dormer, rusticated building stones, and a gang of short, squat columns, and arched windows. The original ticket booth now serves as a bar. Vacationers from San Francisco rode the trains to cottages and small resorts in the valley, while produce, wine, and tons of cobblestones from local quarries were shipped on the rails back to the big growing city for paving Embarcadero and Market Streets.

Rail service to and from Kenwood was discontinued in 1936, and in 1940, the ladies of the Kenwood Improvement Club strong-armed (as only they could) Southern Pacific into selling the depot

Kenwood was for decades the home of the World Pillow Fight Championships, where contestants rode a greased pole over a mud pit, whacking away at each other until one fell off (attracting thousands, the event was moved to the city of Rohnert Park).

## KENWOOD DEPOT

**WHAT:** Sweet, old depot recalls railroad days.

**WHERE:** 314 Warm Springs Rd., Kenwood

**COST:** Free

**PRO TIP:** The main attraction to the Sonoma Valley in the 1900s was natural hot springs; today, seekers of the geothermal waters go to nearby Morton's Warm Springs Resort.

Top left: *On a country road by a vineyard in Kenwood, the restored Kenwood Depot is a sweet antique from the days when narrow-gauge trains arrived in 1886.*

Top right and bottom left: *Stroll around Kenwood Plaza Park to see Victorian-era cottages and mansions, and the circa-1888, white steepled Kenwood Community Church.*

for $10, and today, it's the Kenwood Community Club, the site of many gatherings.

Just up the road, stroll around Kenwood Plaza Park to see Victorian-era cottages and mansions, and the circa-1888, white steepled church. A lesser-known spot for tourists to stop off and relax, here are shaded lawns, a gazebo, a play structure, and picnic tables.

# GEOTHERMAL HOT SPRINGS

## Where can we soak and swim in natural mineral springs?

Attracted to geothermal mineral springs that bubble up from 1,000+ feet below the surface at several locations in what is now Sonoma County, Wappo, Pomo, and Miwok tribespeople in past centuries camped by the warming springs. In the 1880s, escapees from hectic city life climbed aboard trains from San Francisco Bay, headed for a "hot springs" bath house in what is now Glen Ellen. The vacationers set up their tents and lingered for days at a time, immersing themselves in the healing waters. In 1909, a small, rustic lodge and the Los Guilicos Harmonic music pavilion opened to "celebrate old Indian Medicine Springs." A flyer advertised that the resort was "only one mile from the depot over a wild and romantic driveway with half-hourly trips to and from the depot." For $150, you could purchase a lot upon which to build a cottage or erect tents.

Today, the owners of Morton's Warm Springs Resort have discovered arrowheads and artifacts of when the indigenous people enjoyed the springs, as well as remnants of the original stone bath house. Since 1946, on 20 bucolic acres under a canopy of old oak trees, two spring-fed swimming pools and a geothermal wading pool have been popular at Morton's. Families settle in on the picnic grounds, the lounge chairs, and at the snack bar, and when they tire of the pools, they wade in Sonoma Creek.

The springs in Glen Ellen were originally named *Los Guilicos*, after the nearby Wappo village called *Wilikos* on Sonoma Creek.

Top: *Natural geothermal mineral waters flow into the spa's "Watsu" pools and the swimming pools at the Fairmont Sonoma Mission Inn. Photo courtesy of Fairmont Sonoma Mission Inn*

Inset: *Since 1946, under a canopy of old oak trees, two spring-fed swimming pools and a geothermal wading pool have been popular at Morton's Hot Springs, where indigenous people once camped.*

## SONOMA HOT SPRINGS

**WHAT:** Natural, historical thermal mineral springs accessible to visitors in Sonoma Valley

**WHERE:** 1651 Warm Springs Rd., Glen Ellen; as well as other sites

**COST:** Morton's: adults $15, teens and seniors $12, kids 3-12 $8

**PRO TIP:** Just east on Warm Springs Road is the original, restored Kenwood Depot.

In the town of Sonoma, the upscale Fairmont Sonoma Mission Inn welcomes staying guests and daytrippers to enjoy the natural mineral waters that flow into the Willow Stream Spa "Watsu" pools and the swimming pools. Nearby, the thermal, spring-fed swimming pools at Agua Caliente's Sonoma Aquatic Club are open to day use visitors.

# DOWN BY THE TRACKS

## Where is Santa Rosa's old town?

Santa Rosa's Historic Railroad Square looks much as it did in the late 1870s when Northwestern Pacific Railroad trains began to arrive from the shores of San Francisco Bay. Italian stonemasons built the depot and warehouses, canneries, hotels, and breweries, and then rebuilt many of them after the 1906 earthquake. Today, the Sonoma-Marin Area Rail Transit (SMART) arrives at the 1904 depot, which is now a California Welcome Center where you can see memorabilia and vintage photos, and get walking tour maps. Just outside, take selfies with a smiling Charlie Brown and his pal, Snoopy, and with more *Peanuts* characters that turn up in the neighborhood of boutiques, bars, and eateries in the restored buildings.

Among emporiums of curiosities and collectibles is Whistlestop Antiques, in a circa-1920 edifice packed with 10,000 square feet of vintage finds. In the old stone baggage claim building, Aroma Roasters is a refuge for caffeine addicts who are greeted by a mustachioed Snoopy, while Woodstock heralds the tiled entrance to the Omelette Express restaurant. Batcave Comics & Toys lures kids and comics fans into their basement lair, and the impressive stone edifice of the 1907 Hotel La Rose houses the staircase from the San Francisco Cable Car Barn.

Nightlife ensues in a circa-1888 cannery building, where the 6th Street Playhouse puts on plays and musicals, and you can

## HISTORIC RAILROAD SQUARE

**WHAT:** The historic "old town" heart of Santa Rosa

**WHERE:** Bounded by Third, Davis, Wilson, and Sixth Streets

**COST:** Free to see

**PRO TIP:** Nearby SOFA (South of A Street) is a warren of more than 40 art studios and galleries with a BoHo vibe. The annual WinterBlast in this neighborhood includes a sofa parade (literally, sofas).

Top left: *When trains began to arrive in the late 1870s, Italian stonemasons built the depot and warehouses, canneries, hotels, and breweries that today house eateries, boutique shops, and lodgings in the Historic Railroad Square district. Photo courtesy of Sonoma County Library*

Top right: *Snoopy stands in front of the old stone baggage claim building, which is now a coffee house. Photo courtesy of Sonoma County Tourism*

Bottom: *The 1880s water tower at Historic Railroad Square in Santa Rosa, where steam trains once rolled in with passengers from the shores of San Francisco Bay. Photo courtesy of Historic Railroad Square*

listen to jazz and sip local wines by the fireplace at 4th Street Cellars. The elegant 1930s-era bar at Stark's Steak & Seafood wins "Best Happy Hour" awards, and at Jackson's Bar and Oven, "Let That Man Go" and "Stay in Your Lane" cocktails are on the menu.

In the California Welcome Center, kids hang around the scale model train display, complete with tiny trees, historic buildings, and miniature people. Just two blocks away, little ones are also entranced by the baby chicks, fancy hens, and pet rabbits at Western Farm Center, where parents load up on pet supplies.

# A LITTLE RED CHURCH

**How many redwoods does it take to build a church?**

The "Church of One Tree" was constructed in 1873 from a single 275-foot-tall redwood tree, 18 feet in diameter, and comprising 78,000 board feet of lumber. The monster tree was felled and milled near what is now Armstrong Redwoods State Natural Reserve in Guerneville. During the heyday of logging in Northern California, first-growth coast redwoods of those dimensions were just medium-sized, as some top 370 feet, with life spans of 500–700 years.

In a redwood grove at the entrance to Juilliard Park in Santa Rosa, the little red church is a historic landmark, with a tall steeple and the original 19-century stained glass windows. A former First Baptist Church, and believe it or not a former "Ripley's Believe It or Not" museum, it's now a popular rental venue for weddings and events.

## CHURCH OF ONE TREE

**WHAT:** A 19-century architectural gem with an "unbelievable" past

**WHERE:** 492 Sonoma Ave., Santa Rosa

**COST:** Free

**PRO TIP:** A city park since 1931, Juilliard Park has a playground, a bocce court, a community garden, a duck pond, and picnic tables. Although as safe as any city park during daylight hours, it's inadvisable to visit here after dark.

Art lovers wander a block or so to the galleries, studios, and eateries of the South A Street Arts District (SOFA), while garden fanciers head for the nearby Luther Burbank Home and Gardens.

*With a tall steeple and the original 19th-century stained glass windows, the Church of One Tree was, in fact, constructed in 1873 from one 275-foot-tall redwood tree, which was 18 feet in diameter and contained 78,000 board feet of lumber. Photo courtesy of Sonoma County Library*

In about 1959, in rather neglected condition, the building was rolled along the streets from its original downtown site to the current location, where it was completely restored and updated for public use, and is no longer a church.

# SECRET GARDENS

## Where can I learn about garden design?

Tucked away behind a complex of boutique shops and wine-tasting salons on the outskirts of Sonoma Valley is a collection of contemporary-design demonstration gardens, enhanced by some rather dramatic outdoor sculptures and artworks. Dreamed up by the iconic garden-lover's magazine, *Sunset*, nearly a dozen "Test Gardens" are the unique masterpieces of landscape architects and designers from around the world.

In the shimmering White Cloud space, cumulous clouds draped in crystals sparkle above an oyster shell desert dotted with prickly pear cactus. Crowded with bug, bee, and butterfly attractors, the pollinator garden blooms with salvia, verbena, asters, and many more pollen-laden plants. The raised beds in the Farm Garden "allotment" overflow all year with seasonal veggies, pumpkins and sweet peas climb the trellises, and a meandering path leads to the fruit orchard. The kids head for the brightly colored bird and owl boxes and inviting nooks and crannies in the Children's Garden, while their parents relax on sofas amid the herbal plantings in the Cocktail Garden. Among the shops, Potter Green & Co. displays home and garden items created by local artisans, from water features to oversized plant containers, firepits, bird baths, and wind chimes.

Avid foodies and garden lovers gather on the sprawling patio for demos and talks by professional chefs and horticulturalists.

---

Locally grown, organic produce is the foundation of Folktable, the casual, on-site eatery with tables under the trees.

Top: *Luscious succulents are on display in the greenhouse of the Farm Garden at Cornerstone.*

Bottom: *Garden fanciers come across dramatic art installations amid Cornerstone's demonstration gardens in Sonoma Valley.*

## CORNERSTONE

**WHAT:** Unusual gardens hidden behind an open-air marketplace

**WHERE:** 23570 Arnold Dr., Sonoma

**COST:** Free

**PRO TIP:** Watch for the larger-than-life-sized, bright-red Adirondack chair at the turn into Cornerstone.

# FIELD OF DREAMS

## Where can we taste wine and watch baseball?

They built it and we came, to the only regulation-sized baseball field at a winery. With as much romance and goose bump–inducing atmosphere as in the *Field of Dreams* movie, even though the diamond is surrounded by vineyards instead of an Iowa cornfield, the baseball diamond was the bright idea of Balletto Winery's vineyard workers, who also built it. Today, it's the home field for Los Uveros, or The Grapers, who play against other local teams on Sunday mornings. Tuesdays and Thursdays are usually practice days, but spectators are welcome to watch.

Enhancing the winery's sustainable agricultural practices is their location adjacent to the vast Laguna de Santa Rosa wetlands, habitat for myriad species of waterfowl and animals. The winery's

## BALLETTO WINERY

**WHAT:** Baseball and sustainable grape-growing equals fine wines and home runs.

**WHERE:** 5700 Occidental Rd., Santa Rosa

**COST:** Fees for wine tasting and special events

**PRO TIP:** Ask for a map of the self-guided vineyard tour that explains how sustainable practices and terroir affect grape growing. The short walk also leads to the baseball field and the gate to the Laguna footpath.

In the meadow, settle into an Adirondack chair while you sip chardonnay or pinot noir and listen to live music on Saturday afternoons.

Top: *The Field of Dreams baseball field at Balletto Winery in Santa Rosa.* Photo courtesy of Sonoma County Tourism

Bottom: *The tasting terrace at Balletto Winery.* Photo courtesy of Balletto Winery

native wildflower meadow has a gate that accesses the Laguna footpath, a 1.8-mile, flat walking trail through grasslands and a marshy world of vernal pools, riparian woodland, and valley oak savannah rich with wildlife and native flora. Visitors often come for the wine tasting, take the self-guided vineyard tour, and then walk their dogs (on leash) on the trail.

# SLOT CARS, SCIENCE, GAMES, AND TRAINS

**Where can kids go for indoor fun and learning?**

Not just a toy and hobby store, Fundemonium in Rohnert Park is a 14,000-square-foot family play center that hosts daily hands-on activities for kids, from crafts and game playing to slot car and radio-controlled (RC) car racing. For small fees, kids can play a variety of table games, and it's free on "Momnificent Mondays" for little ones to fool around with trains, Legos, blocks, and a play kitchen and grocery store.

Makers love the boat, auto, and plane model kits, as well as all the art supplies. Science nerds head for the electronics and science kits, STEM-based educational items, and robotics. A giant EB-209 RoboCop stands guard at the entrance to the store!

## FUNDEMONIUM

**WHAT:** Interactive play and vehicle racing at a toy and game emporium

**WHERE:** 579 Rohnert Park Expy. W, Rohnert Park

**COST:** Free to watch, with fees for supervised game playing and race tracks

**PRO TIP:** Not enough fun yet? Try the roller blading and roller skating at Cal Skate, just five minutes away in Rohnert Park.

A few minutes away, Rebounderz Indoor Trampoline Park in Rohnert Park sports 75 trampoline beds, an elevated Ninja course, an Xtreme jump tower, indoor playgrounds, and many more uber-stimulating play structures. Parents hang out in their own lounge with Wi-Fi.

Top: *Radio controlled car racing at Fundemonium, a family toy store and play center in Rohnert Park.*

Bottom left: *Kids love the boat, auto, and plane model kits.*

Bottom right: *Toys and games are abundant too.*

An undulating, raucous race track is busy with RC vehicles that dig, fly, float, and race at up to 70 miles an hour—a great spectator sport (bring your own or rent the cars, including the newest models of Corvettes and Broncos). Reservations are required for RC, slot car racing, and "Rock Crawling."

The annual Train Show shows off model trains, all the train set parts, and elaborate miniature scenery, while a steady schedule of events includes Monster Truck–Building RC Camp, Dungeons and Dragons nights, model club meetings, and more.

# MILITARIA ON PARADE

## Where can we learn about military history?

For more than 25 years, the Military Antiques and Museum has exhibited, purchased, and sold memorabilia from the Civil War to the present day, with an emphasis on World War I and World War II. Within the 4,000-square-foot basement of the Petaluma Antique Collective emporium, the military store is jam-packed with uniforms and headgear, deactivated firearms, vintage photos and posters, medals, and much more.

In the aviation section, you'll find flight suits, patches, and goggles, as well as plane models, while a library of several thousand history and reference books makes for irresistible browsing. Shoppers hunt for memorabilia related to their families' experiences in the military, including the Korean and Vietnam conflicts. Collectors dig for hard-to-find antiques such as World War II Soviet and swastika-

Upstairs, the crowded Petaluma Collective curiosity shop contains the wares of 24 antiques dealers, selling everything from advertising signs to vintage clothing, movie posters, LPs, toys, and bric-a-brac.

At the Military Antiques & Museum in Petaluma, vintage uniforms, firearms, photos and posters, medals, and much more recall and honor all the branches of the military.

adorned German war trophies, and personal items used by soldiers in the Spanish-American War and the Civil War.

With a focus on the human side of war via letters, art, and personal items belonging to the common soldier, a museum within the store honors Petaluma's own Sgt. Richard A. Penry, Medal of Honor recipient for extreme heroism in the Vietnam War. His uniform, Medal of Honor, and story are on view in a special display.

# HIDDEN HOUSES

## Where did you say those houses were?

Most travelers drive along Highway 1 enjoying the view of the legendary rugged coastline, never realizing that more than 2,000 homes are hidden in the meadows and behind hedgerows on both sides of the road for about 10 miles stretching down the coast. One of the most restrictive residential developments ever built in the state, Sea Ranch is iconic for its untouched open space and architectural restraint. Widely scattered, naturally weathered, unpainted, contemporary minimalist wooden houses on the headlands and hillsides are barely visible; none are more than two stories tall, and some have sod roofs. Vehicles are out of sight, fences are absent, and native grasses and trees are unfettered by nonindigenous flora. The result of these extraordinary regulations is precious headlands and wooded hills that look much as they did a century ago.

## SEA RANCH

**WHAT:** An architectural landmark, seacoast beaches, and walking trails

**WHERE:** 60 Sea Walk Dr., 20 miles north of Jenner

**COST:** Free

**PRO TIP:** The Sea Ranch Golf Course is open to the public.

Many of the homes at Sea Ranch are available as vacation rentals, with access to swimming pools, tennis courts, a basketball court, a playground, and private trails. Be prepared to share the habitat with deer and fox, wild turkeys, and raccoons!

*Iconic for their untouched open space and architectural restraint, Sea Ranch homes blend into the headlands above the sea. Photo courtesy of James Alinder*

You can get a taste of the "live lightly on the land" concept of The Sea Ranch, along with zowie sea views from walking trails that lead to beaches and along the bluffs, and from paved roads on the east side of the highway that wind through a redwood, madrone, fir, and pine forest, where wild azaleas, rhododendrons, and irises bloom in spring. You can also experience the property from Gualala Point Regional Park, where the Bluff Trail connects to The Sea Ranch coastal access trail.

# ART IN PARADISE

## Where is a sculpture garden with a view?

Striding into the meadow like the Colossus of Rhodes, a looming, elaborately adorned silver figure at Paradise Ridge Winery leads the way to the outdoor art installations that make this place famous. Amid a wooded glen of gnarled oaks and grasslands, several permanent and revolving collections of artworks are connected by walking trails. One of the monumental sculptures is the 34-foot-tall, 25 feet in diameter *Temple of Remembrance*, created in intricate webs of welded steel, within which visitors wander in the flickering light and attach ribbons in remembrance of lost loved ones.

Known for his kinetic sculptures, local artist, Ned Kahn, is represented here with his trembling *Wind Curtain*, and a stainless-steel ring called *Encircled Cloud* from which mist billows mysteriously into a grove of live oaks. At the heart of the sculpture gardens is the reddish steel word "LOVE" in what is called *Marijke's Grove*, in honor of the late Marijke Byck, the art-loving matriarch of the family that owns and operates the winery.

Above the sculpture gardens, the rambling, indoor/outdoor hospitality and wine-tasting edifice was rebuilt after a 2017 firestorm with winds of 80 miles an hour destroyed the original building. On the expansive new verandas and terraces at "Wines & Sunsets," the most popular of wine-tasting events that are

Ironically, following its appearance at Burning Man in 2011, the 12-foot-tall "Love" sculpture was installed permanently at the winery, whereupon it survived the devastating 2017 fire and became a symbol of hope for the county.

Top left and right: *At Paradise Ridge Winery, the* Four Times Daily *sculpture by Robert Ellison stands high above the city of Santa Rosa.*

Inset: *Dana Albany is the creator of* Passage, *representing relationships between mankind, the mechanical, and nature, on view at Paradise Ridge Winery.*

## PARADISE RIDGE WINERY

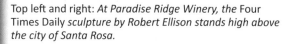

**WHAT:** A vast sculpture garden and winery overlooking the Santa Rosa Plain

**WHERE:** 4545 Thomas Lake Harris Dr., Santa Rosa

**COST:** Free to see; fees for wine tasting and special events

**PRO TIP:** You may well see a herd of 70 or so sheep wandering the vineyards and the sculpture gardens, helping to enrich the soil and prevent fires.

offered, visitors settle in, listen to live music, taste award-winning wines, and nosh on gourmet fare from food trucks, while watching the sun set over the vineyards and the art alfresco.

# STOMPING THE GRAPE

## How can we turn our feet red and celebrate the harvest?

Well, it wouldn't be the Wine Country without a grape stomp at harvesttime, and come October, you'll have ample opportunity to watch wine splattering the denizens of this county and get into the fun yourselves. The "World Championship Grape Stomp" takes place at the Sonoma County Harvest Fair, where costumed competitors get wild, crazy, and dripping with purple, as do some of the spectators. In a barrel half-full of red grapes, the stomper tramps up and down in bare feet, squishing out the juice, which is measured, and the "swabby" stands below the barrel, pulling grape skins and seeds away to keep the juice flowing. Besides bragging rights, the winning team gets a grand prize of more than $1,000. Wine and home brew competitions are also on the menu, along with music and food.

On a late September weekend at the Valley of the Moon Vintage Festival in the Sonoma Plaza, lively grape stomping happens in the amphitheater, with an audience of cheering fans. Calm yourselves from the melee by walking from booth to booth all day, trying the wines of dozens of local wineries, noshing on picnic fare from barbecued oysters to local cheeses, and listening to live music. Stay on for the firefighters' water fights and the lighted parade in the evening.

## HARVEST HIJINKS

**WHAT:** Harvesttime fun in your bare feet

**WHERE:** 1350 Bennett Valley Rd., Santa Rosa (for the Sonoma County Harvest Fair)

**COST:** Fees for wine tasting

**PRO TIP:** 5k, 12k, and Tiny Tots footraces are among the fundraising festivities at the Valley of the Moon Vintage Festival.

*On a late September weekend at the Valley of the Moon Vintage Festival in the Sonoma Plaza, lively grape stomping riles up, and splatters, the crowd. Photos courtesy of Valley of the Moon Vintage Festival*

Among other wineries, Larson Family Winery welcomes visitors to roll up their pants and get into the fun of stomping (and wagon rides) at their Hello Harvest party, while at Bartholomew Estate Winery, you can work off your wine-infused malaise on the Grape Stomp and You-Walk Miwok Loop hiking trail, a challenging, 2.4-mile loop in the oak woodlands.

For a family reunion or a teambuilding group, look into the Sonoma Adventures private grape stomp party; knee-deep in grape juice, the stomper and swabby can't fail to bond.

# MULTICULTURAL MUSEUM

## Where are the Pomo baskets?

Guarded by two black dog sculptures at the entrance, the Santa Rosa Junior College (SRJC) Multicultural Museum houses a truly world-class assemblage of basketry and artifacts from cultures around the world, with an emphasis on local Native American work. Dating from the late 19th century to the 1980s, the Elsie Allen Pomo Basket Collection is the rare and dazzling heart of the museum.

An indigenous people of California from among 70 tribes speaking seven Pomo languages at the time of first European contact, the Pomo lived across much of Northern California. Recognized worldwide today for their unusual techniques of plaiting, coiling, and twining, the baskets were once used for cooking, storing, performing ceremonies, fishing, and carrying babies. The extensive museum collection comes with documentation on the weavers who created them, their relationships to each other, and the materials used in the baskets—mainly willow, bulrush, woolly sedge, and California redbud, all found in and around marshes and streams.

---

### SANTA ROSA JUNIOR COLLEGE MULTICULTURAL MUSEUM

**WHAT:** One of the rarest and largest collections of Native American basketry in the world

**WHERE:** 1501 Mendocino Ave., Santa Rosa

**COST:** Free

**PRO TIP:** Modeled after the Newfoundland breed, the black dog sculptures at the museum were cast in about 1850. Owned by San Franciscans and damaged in the 1906 earthquake, they were sent to Santa Rosa for repair, and the owners never claimed them. The repair company owners saved the iron dogs from being melted down in a scrap drive during World War II by loaning them to SRJC, where they remain.

172

Top left: *Two Newfoundland-style iron dogs guard the entrance to the Santa Rosa Junior College Multicultural Museum.*

Top right: *Twined Pomo baskets from the Klamath River region of Northern California.*

Bottom: *An exceptional exhibit of Puebloan pottery from the Southwest. Photos courtesy of Santa Rosa Junior College Multicultural Museum*

The museum has also enlarged its exhibits of basketry from native cultures across the country and the world, from Puebloan pottery by Maria Martinez to beadwork, ancient Mesoamerican pottery, and art and cultural objects from Asia, Africa, the Pacific Islands, and beyond.

Author of *Pomo Basketmaking: A Supreme Art for the Weaver*, Elsie Allen was the most prolific and influential creator of Pomo basketry. She regularly demonstrated basket weaving and made many educational presentations. Between 1969 and 1971, she completed an astonishing 54 baskets.

During the Depression, the SRJC president and county resident, Jesse Peter, received a WPA grant to build the museum in 1938. From a pioneer family, born in 1885, Peter collected Native American artifacts on his own property and served as the museum's first curator.

# CROSSING THE ART SPECTRUM

## Where will we find the most fine art in one place?

In an unlikely location en route to the Russian River, a warehouse-like building houses the studios of nearly two dozen Sonoma County artists and artisans creating everything from paintings, prints, and sculpture to glassblown pieces, woodworked items, jewelry and more. Fulton Crossing studios are open to the public on weekends, as are three lofty showroom galleries.

Thousands of square feet of antiques are part of the assembly, as is a sprawling showcase of mid-century modern furnishings and accessories, with some art deco added (how about a hula dancer lamp, an Ildefonso Pueblo pot, or Hollywood Regency lounge chairs—no doubt lounged-in by Marilyn Monroe).

Some of the artists at Fulton Crossing are on the annual Sonoma County Art Trails event, said to be the oldest juried open studio tour in the country, and a rare opportunity to hobnob with about 140 juried professional artists who open their studios to the public over two weekends in the fall.

The Fulton Crossing warehouse originally served as a fruit and vegetable packing plant in the 1800s, and then became a winery, a poultry plant, housing for circus animals, and a farmer's market. Look across the road, and you'll see a fresh produce stand, a perfect stop for provisions on the way to picnicking along the Russian River.

Top left: *The artist Beth Failor works in her studio at Fulton Crossing.*

Top right: *The lofty galleries at Fulton Crossing are perfect venues for large art installations.*

Left inset: *A neon sign at the mid-century modern gallery at Fulton Crossing.*

Right inset: *California poppies and seascapes reflect the natural landscape of Sonoma County.*

Another annual art-related event is Sonoma Plein Air Festival, when about three dozen juried artists come from around the country to paint around the county for a week and then show their paintings in the Sonoma Plaza on the weekend—attracting a crowd of avid art collectors.

# LITTLE BITTY TREES

## Where are the pygmies?

Redwood trees are among the world's tallest living things, and yet in the Pygmy Forest on the Sonoma Coast, within Salt Point State Park, redwoods are tiny, only a few feet tall. Along with Bolander pines and Monterey cypress, they are mature, at least a century old, and although they are gnarled and stunted, the trees are miniature versions of their normal cousins—which normally can be 100 feet tall. Created by tectonic and ocean movement eons ago, acidic hardpan soil with few nutrients and poor drainage are the culprits here, preventing the trees from setting roots.

An easy, 3.8-mile loop trail takes you to 1,000 feet in elevation through a lush fern canyon, prairie meadows, and spooky woods of dwarf, bonsai-like plants and trees. A five-year-old cypress, for instance, may be only eight inches tall and have a trunk of less than one inch in diameter.

## PYGMY FOREST

**WHAT:** A rare, fairytale-like miniature forest threaded with footpaths

**WHERE:** 25050 Hwy. 1, Jenner

**COST:** $8 parking fee

**PRO TIP:** Bursting into oceans of pink blooms in late spring, Kruse Rhododendron State Natural Reserve is nearby, on the northern border of the state park.

Mushroom foragers haunt these trails, where many varieties of fungi are found. Unlike elsewhere where foraging is illegal or a fee is charged, there is no fee to pick them here, up to three pounds a day.

*Wander through a lush fern canyon, prairie meadows, and spooky woods of dwarf, bonsai-like plants and trees in a "pygmy forest" at Salt Point State Park.*

Wildflowers decorate the trail, and pileated woodpeckers provide entertainment, along with interpretive signs describing the flora and how it was used by the Kashaya Pomo indigenous people.

Found at the highest elevation within Salt Point State Park, at about 1,000 feet, the elfin evergreen trees are rarely more than three or four feet high; right nearby, the same tree species may be as tall as high-rise buildings.

# CORK-POPPING HISTORY

### How did Francis Korbel get out of jail?

Francis Korbel walked out of jail, smoking a cigar and wearing the clothes that his mom (some say his grandmother) brought when she visited him in prison. The Korbel family and historians claim that Francis, in Prague in 1848, fired the shot that started a revolution against the Austro-Hungarian Empire, and he was imprisoned. After his escape, Korbel sailed to New York City, where he became a cigar-maker, then headed to San Francisco and got into the lumber business, which took him and his brothers to the Russian River valley, where they turned to grape growing and wine making.

By the late 1800s, Korbel Champagne Cellars was an award-winning, internationally recognized producer of méthode champenoise-style sparkling wine, and today it remains the oldest continually operating champagne house in North America. In a bucolic setting in a redwood grove near the Russian River, Korbel offers one of the most rewarding winery experiences in the county, including a museum of vintage photos and artifacts, a film, an in-depth explanation of production, and tastings of the bubbly. Among the compound of historic buildings, the visitors'

Why is Korbel allowed to use the term "champagne" when other wineries, except those in the Champagne region of France, are limited to "sparkling wine"? The 2005 agreement between the United States and the European Union allows bubbly producers to continue to use the term champagne only if they were using it before the date of the agreement.

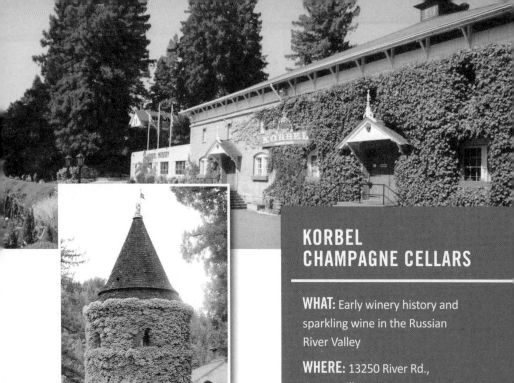

## KORBEL CHAMPAGNE CELLARS

**WHAT:** Early winery history and sparkling wine in the Russian River Valley

**WHERE:** 13250 River Rd., Guerneville

**COST:** Free to see and for three wine tastings; $10–$15 for other tasting programs

**PRO TIP:** Commemorative bottles of Korbel Russian River Valley Natural Champagne were popped at the White House at the inaugurations of Obama, Reagan, Clinton, and Bush.

Top: *The Korbel Champagne Cellars visitors' center was once a Northwestern Pacific train station, one of several in the Russian River Valley in the 1800s.*

Inset: *A landmark amid a compound of historic buildings, the massive, ivy-covered tower at Korbel Champagne Cellars is a replica of one in the former Bohemia, the homeland of the winery's founder, Francis Korbel. Photo courtesy of Korbel Champagne Cellars*

center was once a train station, and the massive, ivy-covered tower is a replica of one in the former Bohemia.

Save a half hour or so to stroll the gardens of the Victorian-era house, which is encircled by 250+ varieties of roses, oceans of spring-blooming bulbs, and a rare redwood hedge. Picnic fare is on offer at the on-site deli, where you can settle in on the deck, with a dazzling vineyard and forest view, and a glass—perhaps a bottle—of the good stuff.

# MAY THE FORCE BE WITH YOU

### Why do *Star Wars* fans go to Petaluma?

As the world's largest privately owned collection of *Star Wars* memorabilia (according to Guinness World Records), Rancho Obi-Wan is a 9,000-square-foot wonderland of action figures, movie props, models, original costumes, posters, video games, and more, much more, with a focus on vintage collectibles from 1977 through 1986.

Fans often make return pilgrimages, as it's impossible to see it all in one visit. In room after room, from floor to ceiling, nearly half a million items include original costumes, models of the Death Star, Funko Pop! vinyls, Ewok and Princess Leia cookie jars, samurai stormtroopers—shall I go on? Dozens of sculptures, recreations, and paintings by fans themselves are part of the fun too.

## RANCHO OBI-WAN

**WHAT:** More *Star Wars* memorabilia than anywhere else in the galaxy

**WHERE:** Directions given when tour is booked

**COST:** Free for ages 12 and under

**PRO TIP:** A nonprofit organization, the museum is open by appointment only; you may need to book weeks in advance for this popular attraction.

The Rancho Obi-Wan owner, and a *Star Wars* collector for more than four decades, Steve Sansweet formerly worked for Lucasfilm as the director of content management and head of fan relations.

*Fans make pilgrimages to Rancho Obi-Wan, the world's largest privately owned collection of* Star Wars *memorabilia in the world, collected over four decades by a former Head of Fan Relations for Lucasfilm. Photos courtesy of Rancho Obi-Wan*

Beyond the movie memorabilia is a library of *Star Wars*–related books, plus toys, musical instruments, and promotional material. In-depth guided tours are led by docents and sometimes by the owner, Steve Sansweet, which comes in handy, as the huge collection can be overwhelming, and visitors often want to locate their favorite ephemera. If Steve is your guide, ask him to autograph one of his books!

No Sith allowed.

# LAVENDER FIELDS FOREVER

## Where shall I take my lavender-loving friend?

The landscape and the climate of Sonoma County remind many people of Provence, which is only five degrees of latitude apart from here. Just as in France, this region of California is famous for vast wine valleys, olive groves, and lavender farms. From May into July, 5,000+ lavender plants burst into flamboyant purple bloom at Lavender Bee Farm near Petaluma, where during the harvest season, tours are available by appointment. While there, be sure to enter the barn, hanging with aromatic bunches, take a look (at a distance) at the 60 beehives, and pick up some of their very popular lavender honey, which sells out every year.

During Lavender Daze on June and early July weekends at Bees N Blooms at the foot of Taylor Mountain, you can wander through eight different varieties of organically grown lavender in the fields, and around a half-mile-long labyrinth of the sweet-smelling plants. You'll also want to see the beehives, a tree nursery, and vegetable and flower gardens. The annual Lavender U-Cut Experience allows you to harvest your own lavender bunches.

### SONOMA COUNTY LAVENDER FARMS

**WHAT:** The fragrant world of Sonoma County lavender

**WHERE:** 6097 Bennett Valley Rd., Santa Rosa (Matanzas Creek Winery) and others

**COST:** Free; events may require fees

**PRO TIP:** Near the village of Occidental, Lynn's Lavender Garden makes for a lavender-lovers destination. Vineyards and old-growth redwoods are the setting for her sprawling French lavender fields, the production barn, and the whimsical lavender/honey showroom.

*Although June is Lavender Month in Sonoma County, on farms and at wineries, fields of fragrant lavender bewitch visitors throughout the early summer.*

Known for their Sauvignon Blanc and Merlot wines, Matanzas Creek Winery is an idyllic destination for its photogenic, terraced lavender gardens, which are available to tour by appointment. Plan a few hours in order to enjoy the bocce courts, a bit of food and wine pairing, and a browse in the "lavender market."

If you feel exceptionally calm as you stroll blooming lavender fields, there may be a reason for that. A study published in *Frontiers in Behavioral Neuroscience* found that sniffing linalool, an alcohol component of lavender odor, had a similar effect as taking a Valium.

# MUSIC OF THE NIGHT

## Where can we hear live music under the stars?

On warm summer nights, the whole side of the Green Music Center building slips away, a huge screen emerges, and music pours out over a sloping greensward dotted with merrymakers and picnickers. Some of the audience sits in the glowing, golden beechwood interior of Weill Hall, while those on the balcony ring peer down above the performers. One of the most acoustically perfect theaters in the West, the Green Center opened in 2012 with a thrilling performance by the flamboyant pianist, Lang Lang. Since then, the Santa Rosa Symphony and visiting orchestras and chamber quartets have been featured, along with such luminaries as Diana Krall, Pink Martini, Jazz at Lincoln Center Orchestra, the Kronos Quartet, Elvis Costello, a bluegrass festival, the Beach Boys, Chaka Khan, Travis Tritt, and other country performers. Special holiday events such as the Fourth of July Spectacular are sellouts.

## GREEN MUSIC CENTER

**WHAT:** The performing arts center at Sonoma State University

**WHERE:** 1801 E Cotati Ave., Rohnert Park

**COST:** Ticket prices are related to the performances; some events are free.

**PRO TIP:** For lawn seating, you can reserve a table or bring your own picnic, chairs, and blankets; wine, water, and snacks are available to purchase.

The Green Music Center has been named "Best Outdoor Venue" in the county.

*Musical evenings are magical in the summertime on the lawns of the Green Music Center in Rohnert Park. Photos courtesy of Green Music Center*

The cathedral-like, 1,400-seat concert hall was designed to replicate the acoustics and the intimacy of two of the top halls in the world: the historic Grosser Musikvereinssaal in Vienna, and the Seiji Ozawa Hall at Tanglewood in Massachusetts. Seats in the main hall were handmade of steamed beechwood, each with an open back for acoustic neutrality. Above is a choir loft and a balcony with views of the Sonoma Mountains through large windows. As at Tanglewood, the entire back wall of the Green Center slides open, allowing outdoor audiences of up to 10,000 to enjoy live performances under the stars.

# MUSEUM IN A MUSEUM

## Why can't I find the Geyserville history museum?

The village of Geyserville sprung up during the mid-1800s when hot springs were discovered nearby and passenger trains began to arrive with vacationers and such luminaries as Ulysses S. Grant and Teddy Roosevelt. It still looks like an old Western town, lined with false-front buildings and wooden boardwalks. Once a buggy workshop, a tinsmith, then a mortuary, and a hardware store, Bosworth & Son General Merchandise on the two-block-long main street remains a hub of community life, as it has since 1911. A fourth-generation Bosworth family member will welcome you inside, where century-old signage and antiques create a turn-of-the-century feel to the store that features Stetson hats and Western shirts, cowboy boots, locally made lariat rope baskets, toys, and rodeo fancy belts.

In the 1903 former bank building on the corner, step in to see the gorgeous teller booths and the vault in the Meeker Vineyard wine-tasting salon.

Top left: *The Geyserville Historical Society museum is tucked away in a village of the mid-1800s.*

Top right, bottom left, and center: *Cowboy boots and hats on sale at Bosworth & Son General Merchandise in Geyserville.*

Bottom right: *The "Geyserville Sculpture Trail" larger-than-life-size art works in meadows along the roadside.*

Walk through the store into the Geyserville Historical Society museum of local and family history, from precious archives to a panoply of vintage photos and posters, and curiosities such as silver spoons pounded out of pre-Civil War 50-cent pieces, a bust of the town's first May Day Queen (she died recently at 103), rare maps, history books, and more.

Wear your Stetson and your boots to the annual Fall Colors and Vintage Car Show in October, which fills both sides of the main street with classic cars, food booths, handmade crafts, and music. Start your day at the fire department's pancake breakfast!

# SOURCES

**Wind beneath Your Wings:** sonomavalleyairport.com; vintageaircraft.com;.airandspace.si.edu/exhibitions/golden-age-flight; historynet.com/curtiss-p-40-warhawk-one-of-ww-iis-most-famous-fighters.htm

**Call of the Wild:** JackLondonPark.com; jacklondonpark.com/wolf-house; transcendencetheatre.org

**Landfill to Landmark:** patrickamiot.com; downtownmarkham.ca/community/carousel/patrick-amiot/; thecommunityvoice.com/article/Creativity-is-contagious

**A Ghostly Forest:** BuenaVistaWinery.com; sonomavalleywine.com/the-roots/history/#.YGyLfx1lD1I. noehill.com/sonoma/cal0392.asp. bartholomewestate.com

**Starstruck at Sugarloaf:** sugarloafpark.org; rfo.org; Dark Sky Week: darksky.org; rfo.org/index.php/planet-walk; winecountrystarparty.com; Sonoma State University Astronomy Department public events: phys-astro.sonoma.edu

**Remembering the _Snark_:** jacklondonyachtclub.org; jacklondonlodge.com; jacklondonpark.com

**Belly Up to the Bar:** washoe.house; stormysrestaurant.com

**The Nicholas Effect:** nicholasgreen.org; parks.sonomacounty.ca.gov/Visit/Coastal-Prairie-Trail; bbc.com/news/magazine-39422660

**Hanging Out with _Peanuts_:** sonomacounty.com/sites/default/files/legacy-files/pdf/PeanutsStatuesAroundTown-LowRes_2-27-15.pdf

**Marine Science on View:** marinescience.ucdavis.edu/bml/visiting-bml

**Flying in the Treetops:** sonomacanopytours.com; savetheredwoods.org/redwoods; nps.gov/redw/learn/nature/threatened-and-endangered-species.htm; sonomamag.com/sleep-in-a-treehouse-then-fly-through-the-redwoods-at-sonomas-newest-glamping-spot

**Historic Heart of Sonoma:** californiafrontier.net/jose-altimira-san-francisco-solano; sonomasun.com/2006/09/21/pub-a-1382

**Movie Mavens' Winery:** francisfordcoppolawinery.com; prnewswire.com/news-releases/francis-ford-coppola-receives-2019-wine-enthusiast-lifetime-achievement-award-300917483.html; facebook.com/WineEnthusiast/posts/over-the-years-francis-ford-coppola-winery-has-added-varietals-or-blends-to-its-/10156157030676923

**No Nukes on This Coast:** yubanet.com/california/signs-of-1906-earthquake-revealed-in-mapping-of-offshore-northern-san-andreas-fault; sonomacounty.com/articles/explore-bodega-head-sonoma-coast; .en.wikipedia.org/wiki/Bodega_Bay_Nuclear_Power_Plant

**Saving Endangered Flora:** sonomabg.org; biologicaldiversity.org/programs/biodiversity/elements_of_biodiversity/extinction_crisis/index.html; nhm.ac.uk/discover/news/2020/september/two-in-five-plants-are-threatened-with-extinction.html; sonomabg.org/acerpentaphyllum.html; sonomabg.org/page26.html

**NASCAR and Drags:** sonomaraceway.com; nascar.com/gallery/sonoma-raceway/#photo-2; searspointracing.com/programs-experiences/go-karting

**Plant Wizard's Garden:** lutherburbank.org; santarosahistory.com/wordpress/2020/10/everybody-wants-a-piece-of-luther-burbank; csmonitor.com/1987/1021/uluth.html; wschs.org/farm

**The Apple Abides:** farmtrails.org/gravenstein-apple-fair/; sonomacounty.com/articles/gravenstein_apples; appleblossomfest.com; fortross.org/lib/109/fort-ross-orchards.pdf; slowfoodusa.org/saving-the-gravensteins; fruitguys.com/2013/07/save-the-gravenstein; momsapplepieusa.com; fruitguys.com/2019/08/eat-the-endangered-gravenstein-apple

**Jets, Copters, Planes:** PacificCoastAirMuseum.org; sonomacounty.com/cultural-arts/pacific-coast-air-museu

**Ridin' a Real Train:** traintown.com; en.wikipedia.org/wiki/Sonoma_TrainTown_Railroad

**On Safari in Sonoma:** safariwest.com

**A Rambling Rancho:** petalumaadobe.com; parks.sonoma.net/adobe.html; nps.gov/nr/travel/ca/ca43.htm; nps.gov/goga/learn/historyculture/spanish-mexican-period.htm

**Plenty of Pliny:** russianriverbrewing.com; seismicbrewingco.com. drinkgoldenstate.com; zythophile.co.uk/2010/03/14/so-what-did-pliny-the-elder-say-about-hops; shop.russianriverbrewing.com/products/pliny-the-elder-12-pk-510-ml-bottles-shipping-in-ca-only

**Hail to the Count!:** buenavistawinery.com; facebook.com/george.webber1; bit.ly/3tM9bHd

**Pedal Your Trolley:** Bikehealdsburg.com; sonomacounty.com/blog/bike-healdsburg-pedal-trolley-lets-you-roll-style?fbclid=IwAR1ItDcvAGJs-2-Rxm-ENL9dA381eYLsAP6DdReG1L-RBAML0C8d4M7xYKA

**Seals and Sea Stacks:** parks.ca.gov/?page_id=451; sonomawater.org/marine-mammals; sfgate.com/bayarea/article/Ice-Age-clues-near-Bodega-Scientist-thinks-2466058.php

**Trains, Teapots, Rodeos:** sonomacounty.ca.gov/PRMD/Planning/Historic-Resources/Duncans-Mills; russianriverrodeo.org

**A Whale of a Time:** baynature.org/article/a-seasonal-whale-finder-for-california; stewardsofthecoastandredwoods.org; parks.sonomacounty.ca.gov; bodegabaysportfishing.com

**Walls with Stories:** openandoutsr.com/art; srcity.org/DocumentCenter/View/18809/Santa-Rosa-Public-Artwalk-Map; srcity.org/760/Downtown-Connect; socoimm.org/public-art/scape/; petalumaartscenter.org; visitpetaluma.com; sonomacounty.com/cultural-arts/south-street-art-district; SouthFirstFridays.com

**Victorian Beauties:** noehill.com/sonoma/nat1974000560.as; rynersonobrien.com/mcdonald/index.html; dearoldhollywood.blogspot.com/2013/07/santa-rosa-california-mcdonald-avenue.html; Ca'Bianca: 835 Second St., Santa Rosa, (707) 544-2258; oldhouseonline.com/house-tours/a-study-of-stick-style; period-homes.com/palladio-awards/1035-2; sfgate.com/bayarea/article/Movie-Row-Santa-Rosa-s-McDonald-Avenue-retains-2787046.php

**Dinos, Rhinos, and Bears:** swedesfeeds@yahoo.com; sciencemag.org/news/2020/12/us-agency-sidesteps-listing-monarch-butterflies-endangered

**The Tsar Loved Sonoma:** fortross.org; Schubert, John C., and Valerie A. Munthe. 2017. "Sea People." In Hidden History of Sonoma County, pg. 44. Cheltenham, UK: History Press

**Here Come the Birds:** innatthetides.com/tides-wharf-restaurant/; imdb.com/title/tt0056869/; dailymail.co.uk/news/article-2079644/Has-mystery-Alfred-Hitchcocks-thriller-The-Birds-finally-solved.html; bodegabay.com/the-birds/; en.wikipedia.org/wiki/The_Birds_(film)

**Nature's Aquariums:** parks.ca.gov/?page_id=451; parks.ca.gov/?page_id=453

**Redwoods and Ravioli:** unionhoteloccidental.com; negrisrestaurant.com; sonomacounty.ca.gov/PRMD/Planning/Historic-Resources/Occidental; occidentalcenterforthearts.org

**Glamping in Style:** autocamp.com; glampinghub.com; safariwest.com

**A Moooving Experience:** parks.sonomacounty.ca.gov/Visit/Tolay-Lake-Regional-Park; parks.sonomacounty.ca.gov/Visit/Helen-Putnam-Regional-Park/; parks.sonomacounty.ca.gov/Play/Tolay-Fall-Festival; parks.sonomacounty.ca.gov/Visit/Taylor-Mountain-Regional-Park-and-Preserve

**Sizzling Retro Regalia:** hotcouturevintage.com; disguisethelimitsr.com; vsvshop.myshopify.com

**Stonelace at the Shore:** sonomacounty.com/outdoor-activities/salt-point-state-park; parks.ca.gov/pages/734/files/GeoGem%20Note%2016%20Salt%20Point%20State%20Park.pdf; worldatlas.com/articles/weathering-landforms-what-is-a-tafoni.html; nps.gov/articles/tafoni.htm

**History on the Plaza:** sonomavalley.com; parks.ca.gov/?page_id=479; sonomavalleywinetrolley.com; sonomacounty.com/cultural-arts/blue-wing-inn; nps.gov/nr/travel/ca/ca44.htm

**Fluttering in the Wind:** nedkahn.com; nedkahn.com/portfolio/microturbines. h2hotel.com/hotel/artwork; pressdemocrat.com/article/news/macarthur-grant-sculptors-air-garden-takes-shape-in-sebastopol; piazzahospitality.com/hotel-sebastopol; ci.sebastopol.ca.us/SebastopolSite/media/Documents/Public_notices/ned_kahn.pdf?ext=.pdf; museumsc.org/kinetics/; sonomawest.com/sonoma_west_times_and_news/news/new-public-art-the-shape-of-things-to-come/article_787e64de-dd30-11e8-98d8-578e9fa77471.html

**The Water Wheel Turns:** Jacklondonvillage.net/jacklondonvillage-glen-ellen-sonoma-history.html; SculptureSite.com; glenellenhistoricalsociety.org; JackLondonPark.com

**Early California History:** californiamissionsmuseum.com; sonomacounty.com/cultural-arts/california-missions-museum

**Food Trucks, Latino Style:** mitotefoodpark.com; instagram.com/charronegrofood; instagram.com/luchasabina; Tacos La Bamba, 18155 Sonoma Hwy. 12, Sonoma; instagram.com/streetsideasiangrill

**A Plea for Peace:** timbercoveresort.com; corvidsketcher.com/2015/01/27/bufano-the-california-coast-and-colma; roadsideamerica.com/story/20796; calexplornia.com/bufano-peace-statue-monument

**Russian Totems:** parks.sonomacounty.ca.gov/Visit/Gualala-Point-Regional-Park; fortross.org/sakha-story.htm; gualalaarts.org; gualalaarts.org/Events/2012-07-Yakut-Totem.html

**The American Dream:** robledofamilywinery.com/Our-Story/Family-Bios; sonomacounty.com/articles/carneros-sonoma-wine-region-and-appellation; si.edu/search?edan_q=Robledo&, americanhistory.si.edu/food/wine-table/la-familia-robledo; airbnb.com/rooms/19054165?source_impression_id=p3_1611866344_vpKiunpgJN4%2Fu7cC

**Founder of Sonoma:** sonomaparks.org/location/general-vallejos-home; parks.ca.gov/?page_id=479; sonomavalley.com/listing/general-mariano-guadalupe-vallejos-home/415; starcraftcustombuilders.com/Architectural.Styles.Victorian.htm; searsarchives.com/homes/1908-1914.htm; redshift.autodesk.com/history-of-prefabrication

**Rhodies in Bloom:** parks.ca.gov/?page_id=448

**The World of *Peanuts*:** schulzmuseum.org; sonomacounty.com/articles/explore-snoopy-and-peanuts-sonoma-county-2-day-itinerary; cmosc.org

**We're Still Here!:** pressdemocrat.com/article/news/muralist-transforms-drab-stretch-of-hopper-avenue-near-coffey-park-in-santa/?artslide=0; muraldecor.com; securitypublicstorage.com/blog/sps-debuts-new-mural-celebrating-oceanside-community

**Giant Redwoods:** parks.ca.gov/?page_id=450; stewardsofthecoastandredwoods.org/index.html; sonomacounty.com/articles/explore-california-redwoods; savetheredwoods.org; sonomacounty.com/outdoor-activities/armstrong-redwoods-state-natural-reserve

**A Green Dream of a Winery:** benziger.com, benziger.com/animals-gardens; sonoma.com/blog/benziger-tribute-tour; cntraveler.com/story/best-restaurants-world

**Oenophiles' Hideaway:** sonomalibrary.org/locations/sonoma-county-wine-library; friendsofthewinelibrary.org; sonomacounty.com/chamber-cvb/healdsburg-chamber-commerce-visitors-bureau

**Sonoma Cable Cars:** sonomavalleywinetrolley.com

**The Old Traders' Trail:** parks.ca.gov. (707) 875-3483; parks.sonoma.net; visitjenner.com/hiking-trails; stewardscr.org/pdf/ELP_Docent_Manual.pdf; digitalassets.lib.berkeley.edu/anthpubs/ucb/text/ucar025-001.pdf; museum.santarosa.edu/elsie-allen-pomo-basket-collection; russianrivergetaways.com/things-to-do/history; stewardscr.org/pdf/SC%20Roving%20Naturalist%20Forms.pdf

**Brain Freeze Is Worth It:** frozenarticecream.com; fru-ta.com; vice.com/en/article/9bdzvd/mexico-tocumbo-land-of-frozen-desserts; culinarybackstreets.com/cities-category/mexico-city/2018/a-treat-from-tocumbo; news-press.com/story/life/food/2015/07/21/michoacana-ice-cream-fort-myers-naples-lehigh-bonita-mexican-dessert/30459837; traderjimsfloats.com/about; nimbleandfinns.com

**West County Charm:** gratoncommunityclub.org; gratoncommunityclub.org/mission-and-history; purplebrands.com/contract-services/#tab-our-facilities-content; bowmancellars.com/visit

**Geological Wonder:** petrifiedforest.org; en.wikipedia.org/wiki/Petrified_Forest_(California); sonomacounty.com/wineries/hans-fahden-winery; hansfahden.com

**Chapel by the Sea:** thesearanchchapel.org; diablotimber.com/blog/sea-ranch-chapel-part-3; ilanlaelfoundation.org/work/the-sea-ranch-chapel; tsra.org

**Blink and You'll Miss It:** cafeaquaticajenner.com; sonomacounty.com/chamber-cvb/jenner-visitors-center; watertreks.com; wildlandsconservancy.org/preserves/jennerheadlands

**Wildlife and Wastewater:** petalumawetlands.org/wetlands; cityofpetaluma.org/water-recycling; colintalcroft.com/Sonoma_County_Bird_Watching_Spots/Shollenberger_Park_Petaluma.html

**Running with Christo:** museumsc.org/tom-golden-collection; en.wikipedia.org/wiki/Running_Fence#/media/File:ChristoMarker3185.jpg; americanart.si.edu/exhibitions/christo

**Redwoods on the Fairway:** northwoodgolf.com; camoupedia.blogspot.com/2014/07/the-link-between-golf-and-camouflage.html; top100golfcourses.com/golf-course/northwood-golf-club

**Japanese-Style Serenity:** osmosis.com, osmosis.com/blog/tag/sound-healing, osmosis.com/blog/days-of-wines-and-enzymes, osmosis.com/press; robertketchell.com/about; experienceispa.com/ispa-academy/glossary-terms/item/japanese-enzyme-bath-2

**Old Railroad Days:** kenwooddepot.com; mortonwarmsprings.com; kenwoodhistory.wordpress.com/2018/02/24/the-hazy-history-of-the-kenwood-depot

**Geothermal Hot Springs:** mortonswarmsprings.com; fairmont.com/sonoma/spa/spa; sonomaaquaticclub.com; docs.cpuc.ca.gov/PUBLISHED/Comment_resolution/103106.htm

**Down by the Tracks:** railroadsquare.net; sonomacounty.com/shopping/santa-rosas-historic-railroad-square; noehill.com/sonoma/nat1979000561.aspx

**A Little Red Church:** srcity.org/633/Church-of-One-Tree; pressdemocrat.com/article/news/srs-one-tree-icon-gets-new-life-thanks-to-patience-hard-work; sonomacounty.com/articles/explore-california-redwoods

**Secret Gardens:** cornerstonesonoma.com; sonomamag.com/find-inspiration-for-your-edible-garden-at-cornerstone-sonoma; sunset.com

**Field of Dreams:** ballettovineyards.com/our-baseball-dream-field; parks.sonomacounty.ca.gov/Visit/Laguna-de-Santa-Rosa-Trail; Trailheads, with parking: 6303 Hwy. 12 and 5420 Occidental Rd.

**Slot Cars, Science, Games, and Trains:** fundemoniumtoys.com; rebounderz.com/city/rohnert-park; calskate.com

**Militaria on Parade:** militaryantiquesmuseum.com

**Hidden Houses:** searanchrentals.com; tsra.org; searanchescape.com; searanchlodge.com; youtube.com/watch?v=hKUHfBfF-3c; nytimes.com/2019/06/11/arts/design/sea-ranch-california.html; stayinsearanch.com/top-5-beaches-in-the-sea-ranch

**Art in Paradise:** prwinery.com; celebratesculpture.com; rgj.com/story/life/arts/2017/10/14/california-fires-burning-man-art-survives-artists-studio-destroyed/762636001; danaalbanyart.com/passagesculpture

**Stomping the Grape:** harvestfair.org; bartholomewestate.com; larsonfamilywinery.com; sonoma-adventures.com/grape-stomp

**Multicultural Museum:** museum.santarosa.edu; foundation.santarosa.edu/hidden-gem-srjc-jesse-peter-multicultural-museum; pressdemocrat.com/article/news/legendary-pomo-basket-maker-elsie-allen-defied-tradition-to-preserve-it; museum.santarosa.edu/yandle-dogs

**Crossing the Art Spectrum:** fultoncrossing.com; sonomacountyarttrails.org/artists; sonomapleinair.com

**Little Bitty Trees:** parks.ca.gov/?page_id=453; sonomacounty.com/articles/salt-point-state-parks-pygmy-forest-gualala; parks.ca.gov/?page_id=448; modern-forager.com/salt-point-state-park-february/; theoutbound.com/san-francisco/chillin/bolete-mushroom-hunting

**Cork-Popping History:** Korbel.com; fundinguniverse.com/company-histories/f-korbel-bros-inc-history; onwardtoourpast.com/genealogy_blog/czech-genealogy/czech-genealogy-the-wonderful-story-of-the-amazing-bohemian-korbel-brothers-installment-1-of-2.html; winc.com/blog/difference-champagne-sparkling-wine; wineoh.tv/sonoma-champagne-served-at-inauguration

**May the Force Be with You:** info@ranchoobiwan.org, ranchoobiwan.com.

**Lavender Fields Forever:** matanzascreek.com; lavenderbeefarm.com; beesnblooms; micheleannajordan.com/article/narrative/sonoma-americas-provence; nytimes.com/2018/10/23/science/lavender-scent-anxiety.html; (707) 874-9960, lynnslavender.com

**Music of the Night:** gmc.sonoma.edu; gmc.sonoma.edu/our-venues/weill-hall; rsconstruction.com/projects/csu-sonoma-green-music-center

**Museum in a Museum:** bosworthandson.com; sonomawest.com/the_healdsburg_tribune/news/geyserville-s-bosworth-store-is-retiring-into-history/article_b7b38e74-ce52-11e7-b2cf-075405e9cc21.html; pressdemocrat.com/article/news/more-than-just-a-shop-bosworth-and-son-opens-geyservillehistory-museum/?artslide=2

# INDEX